THEIR HEARTS BURNED

THEIR
HEARTS
BURNED

WALKING WITH JESUS ALONG THE EMMAUS ROAD:
AN EXCURSION THROUGH THE OLD TESTAMENT

Kevin O'Donnell

MONARCH
BOOKS

Oxford, UK & Grand Rapids, Michigan, USA

First published in the UK in 2006 by Monarch Books (a publishing
imprint of Lion Hudson plc), Mayfield House, 256 Banbury Road,
Oxford OX2 7DH.
Tel: +44 (0)1865 302750 Fax: +44 (0)1865 302757
Email: monarch@lionhudson.com
www.lionhudson.com

ISBN-13: 978-1-85424-758-2 (UK)
ISBN-10: 1-85424-758-1 (UK)
ISBN-13: 978-0-8254-6117-0 USA)
ISBN-10: 0-8254-6117-0 (USA)

Distributed by:
UK: Marston Book Services Ltd, PO Box 269,
Abingdon, Oxon OX14 4YN;
USA: Kregel Publications, PO Box 2607,
Grand Rapids, Michigan 49501

Unless otherwise stated, Scripture quotations are taken from the
Holy Bible, New International Version, © 1973, 1978, 1984 by the
International Bible Society. Used by permission of Hodder &
Stoughton Ltd. All rights reserved.

The text paper used in this book has been made from wood inde-
pendently certified as having come from sustainable forests.

British Library Cataloguing Data
A catalogue record for this book is available from the British
Library.

Printed and bound in Great Britain by Cox & Wyman Ltd,
Reading.

Contents

Introduction   7

Part 1 – Jesus in the Law of Moses   15
Jesus in Genesis   17
Jesus in Exodus   34
Jesus in Leviticus   50
Jesus in Numbers   59
Jesus in Deuteronomy   65

Part 2 – Jesus in the Historical Books   71
Jesus in Joshua   73
Jesus in Judges   81
Jesus in Ruth   85
Jesus in 1 and 2 Samuel   89
Jesus in 1 and 2 Kings   97

Part 3 – Jesus in the Wisdom Literature   103
Jesus in Job   105
Jesus in the Psalms   110
Jesus in Proverbs   119
Jesus in Ecclesiastes   123
Jesus in the Song of Songs   126

Part 4 – Jesus in the Prophets   131
Jesus in Isaiah   133

Jesus in Jeremiah and Lamentations   141
Jesus in Ezekiel   146
Jesus in Daniel   150
Jesus in Hosea   155
Jesus in Joel   159
Jesus in Amos   162
Jesus in Obadiah   165
Jesus in Jonah   167
Jesus in Micah   169
Jesus in Nahum   172
Jesus in Habakkuk   174
Jesus in Zephaniah   177
Jesus in Haggai   179
Jesus in Zechariah   182
Jesus in Malachi   185

Appendix 1: The Hope of Israel   189
Appendix 2: Oracles about Jesus   203

Introduction

On the road to Emmaus

Now that same day two of them were going to a village called Emmaus, about seven miles from Jerusalem. They were talking with each other about everything that had happened. As they talked and discussed these things with each other, Jesus himself came up and walked along with them; but they were kept from recognising him.

He asked them, 'What are you discussing together as you walk along?'

They stood still, their faces downcast. One of them, named Cleopas, asked him, 'Are you only a visitor to Jerusalem and do not know the things that have happened there in these days?'

'What things?' he asked.

'About Jesus of Nazareth,' they replied. 'He was a prophet, powerful in word and deed before God and all the people. The chief priests and our rulers handed him over to be sentenced to death, and they crucified him; but we had hoped that he was the one who was going to redeem Israel. And what is more, it is the third day since all this took place. In addition, some of our women amazed us. They went to the tomb early this morning but didn't find his body. They came and told us that they had seen a vision of angels, who said he was alive. Then some of our companions went to the tomb and found it just as the women had said, but him they did not see.'

He said to them, 'How foolish you are, and how slow of heart to believe all that the prophets have spoken! Did not the Christ have to suffer these things and then enter his glory?' And beginning with Moses and all the Prophets, he explained to them what was said in all the Scriptures concerning himself.

As they approached the village to which they were going, Jesus acted as if he were going further. But they urged him strongly, 'Stay with us, for it is nearly evening; the day is almost over.' So he went in to stay with them.

When he was at the table with them, he took bread, gave thanks, broke it and began to give it to them. Then their eyes were opened and they recognised him, and he disappeared from their sight. They asked each other, 'Were not our hearts burning within us while he talked with us on the road and opened the Scriptures to us?'

(Luke 24:13–32)

The Hit List

I was listening to a teaching tape some years ago. Various speakers were on it from a US convention. One of them, Oral Roberts, suddenly launched forth with an impressive list of the books of the Old Testament and how Jesus was predicted in each one. It was a *tour de force*, delivered with the rapidity of a machine gun and the spirituality of a thunderbolt. I played that tape back again and again to note down that list, and I still have it to hand today. This is how it goes...

- Genesis – Jesus is the promised seed
- Exodus – Jesus is the Passover lamb
- Leviticus – Jesus is the high priest
- Numbers – Jesus is seen in the fire and the cloud

- Deuteronomy – Jesus is the prophet to come
- Joshua – Jesus is the Captain of the Lord of Hosts
- Judges – Jesus is the ideal judge and lawgiver
- 1 and 2 Samuel – Jesus is the trusted prophet
- 1 and 2 Kings, 1 and 2 Chronicles – Jesus is the reigning king
- Ezra – Jesus is the faithful scribe
- Nehemiah – Jesus is the wall builder
- Esther – Jesus is the greater Mordecai
- Job – Jesus is the living redeemer
- Psalms – Jesus is the shepherd
- Proverbs and Ecclesiastes – Jesus is Wisdom
- Song of Songs – Jesus is the lover and bridegroom
- Isaiah – Jesus is the Prince of Peace
- Jeremiah – Jesus is the Righteous Branch
- Lamentations – Jesus is the weeping prophet
- Ezekiel – Jesus is the four-faced man
- Daniel – Jesus is the fourth man
- Hosea – Jesus is the faithful husband
- Joel – Jesus is the baptizer in the Holy Spirit
- Amos – Jesus is the burden bearer
- Obadiah – Jesus is the one mighty to save
- Jonah – Jesus is the foreign missionary
- Micah – Jesus is the messenger with beautiful feet
- Nahum – Jesus is the avenger of God's elect
- Habakkuk – Jesus is the reviver of the work of God
- Zephaniah – Jesus is the saviour
- Haggai – Jesus is the restorer of ancient heritage
- Zechariah – Jesus is the fountain open in the House of David
- Malachi – Jesus is the sun of righteousness with healing in his wings

The speaker did not stop there – even for a breath! – as he raced on through each book of the New Testament saying what it declared about Jesus; for example, Matthew shows him as the Messiah, Mark as a wonder-worker, Luke as Son of man and John as Son of God.

Setting the Precedent

This was striking and edifying, and it echoes the passage quoted earlier from Luke 24 about the risen Lord walking on the road to Emmaus with two disciples. He taught them all about the Scriptures, opening these up to their spirits and revealing what each of the books had to say about him, from Moses and the prophets right through. They were blasted in the gut with Holy Spirit revelation and wisdom, saying how their hearts felt as though they were burning within them. Jesus himself set the precedent for reading the Old Testament in the light of his life. The early Christians followed suit and ransacked the old Scriptures for any clues and insights about Jesus. Let us remember that for the first believers, their only Scriptures were those of the Old Testament, the Hebrew Bible or the Greek translation, the Septuagint. The Gospels and epistles came later, formed gradually during the first century AD. By the end of the century they were copied, widely circulated and revered. Any documents that came from the apostles or contained the words of the Lord were so revered and copied. However, the first believers had the Old Testament to work with and a rich tapestry of ideas and images were drawn from this and seen as pointers to Christ. Bible scholars such as C.H. Dodd declared that the Old Testament was 'the substructure of New Testament theology.'[1]

Jewish Techniques

There are obvious oracles, predictions about the Messiah in the Old Testament. To interpret these in the light of Jesus is fine, but some would say that to see references to Jesus in various details and stories that are not so obvious might be reading things into the text, a case of wishful thinking or seeing faces in the coals of a fire. Thus, to say that Isaac carrying the wood up Mount Moriah for the sacrifice (Genesis 22:6) is a type of Christ carrying the cross raises some eyebrows but I would argue that there are many such riches to be discovered in there and this follows the style of interpretation set out by first century Jews. The first Christians were Jews and Jewish tradition at the time of Jesus reveals a wealth of techniques that the rabbis had for reading and interpreting Scripture. These ways were quite imaginative, flexible, playful even, and we can see them utilized in early Christian exposition. They had five main ways of interpreting the Scriptures besides the obvious, historical or literal reading of a story or passage. They drew ideas out and expanded on them in translation or in retelling, they seized on special words that seemed to resonate with present significance, or they saw hidden symbols and allegories. Thus, Jesus expanded on the story of the heavenly manna in the wilderness in John 6 about the bread of life:

Our forefathers ate the manna in the desert; as it is written: 'He gave them bread from heaven to eat.'

---

1. C.H. Dodd, *According to the Scriptures: The Substructure of New Testament Theology*, 1952

Jesus said to them, 'I tell you the truth, it is not Moses who has given you the bread from heaven, but it is my Father who gives you the true bread from heaven. For the bread of God is he who comes down from heaven and gives life to the world.'

'Sir,' they said, 'from now on give us this bread.'

Then Jesus declared, 'I am the bread of life. He who comes to me will never go hungry, and he who believes in me will never be thirsty...

'Stop grumbling among yourselves,' Jesus answered. 'No-one can come to me unless the Father who sent me draws him, and I will raise him up at the last day. It is written in the Prophets: "They will all be taught by God." Everyone who listens to the Father and learns from him comes to me. No-one has seen the Father except the one who is from God; only he has seen the Father. I tell you the truth, he who believes has everlasting life. I am the bread of life. Your forefathers ate the manna in the desert, yet they died. But here is the bread that comes down from heaven, which a man may eat and not die. I am the living bread that came down from heaven. If anyone eats of this bread, he will live for ever. This bread is my flesh, which I will give for the life of the world.'

Look at Exodus 34:29–35 and the glory of God shining out from the face of Moses. Compare 2 Corinthians 3:17–18 when the glory shines from the faces of believers who are in the Spirit. Paul is expanding upon the Exodus verses:

When Moses came down from Mount Sinai with the two tablets of the Testimony in his hands, he was not aware that his face was radiant because he had spoken with the Lord. When Aaron and all the Israelites saw Moses, his face was radiant, and they were afraid to come near him. But Moses called to them; so Aaron and all the leaders of the community came back to him, and he spoke to them. Afterwards all the Israelites came near him, and he gave them all the commands the Lord had given him on Mount Sinai.

When Moses finished speaking to them, he put a veil over his face. But whenever he entered the Lord's presence to speak with him, he removed the veil until he came out. And when he came out and told the Israelites what he had been commanded, they saw that his face was radiant. Then Moses would put the veil back over his face until he went in to speak with the Lord.   (Exodus 34:29–35)

This is used in the New Testament thus:

Now the Lord is the Spirit, and where the Spirit of the Lord is, there is freedom. And we, who with unveiled faces all reflect the Lord's glory, are being transformed into his likeness with ever-increasing glory, which comes from the Lord, who is the Spirit. (1 Corinthians 3:17–18)

Early Christian writers abounded with suggested symbols or types of Christ in the Old Testament, and these form the backbone of the 'Hit List' of the US preacher mentioned earlier.

Let us search through the Old Testament books and see how they might speak of Jesus so that our hearts may burn within us, also. This is not just an academic exercise in exegesis, but a spiritual blessing, a journey that will refresh the spirit. Look at these words when John had a vision of the risen Jesus in all his glory:

I turned around to see the voice that was speaking to me. And when I turned I saw seven golden lampstands, and among the lampstands was someone 'like a son of man',

dressed in a robe reaching down to his feet and with a
golden sash around his chest. His head and hair were
white like wool, as white as snow, and his eyes were like
blazing fire. His feet were like bronze glowing in a
furnace, and his voice was like the sound of rushing
waters. In his right hand he held seven stars, and out of
his mouth came a sharp double-edged sword. His face
was like the sun shining in all its brilliance.

When I saw him, I fell at his feet as though dead. Then
he placed his right hand on me and said: 'Do not be
afraid. I am the First and the Last. I am the Living One; I
was dead, and behold I am alive for ever and ever! And I
hold the keys of death and Hades.'   (Revelation 1:12–18)

Let the sound of his voice wash over you and through you
like the sound of roaring waters. May his beauty and his
grace be opened up to you. May that blessing be with you
and upon you as you read. Make this a voyage of discov-
ery, letting the pages of the Old Testament come alive in a
new, relevant way.

PART ONE –
Jesus in the Law
of Moses

The books of the Torah, the Law, are foundational for Jewish faith. Besides many ceremonial and ritual laws, there are abiding ethical codes as well as stories of the ancestors and heroes of the faith. We can trawl through these five books, Genesis, Exodus, Leviticus, Numbers and Deuteronomy, to find many rich references to Jesus.

Jesus in Genesis

In the Beginning
Genesis takes us to the very beginning of the Bible and
the start of God's plan for the earth. It explains how
creation fell into sin and decay and there are seeds of
hope for a new beginning. Jesus is prefigured as

* The Word
* The seed
* The ark
* The sacrifice
* The ruler

The Word

The Power of Words
We speak about 'keeping our word' or 'giving our word'. If
we are honourable, then we do so. To the Hebrew mind,
your word was your innermost being, your heart and
thoughts, your energy and drive, brought out, spoken by
the lips and made manifest. Its power was in the very
expression of who you were. Thus the word of a king was
binding, and the word of God spoken by a prophet was
sacred. Words had power in themselves, a derived power
from the one who expressed them. They were 'you' out in
the open.

Words are still seen as powerful in modern times. Psychology agrees that the words spoken about us can build up or pull down. The old nursery rhyme, 'Sticks and stones may break my bones, but words can never harm me' is a lie. Words can wound the spirit, or encourage us greatly. Children who are not praised do not flourish; self-esteem suffers. A father scolded and reprimanded a child many times over for being clumsy, not good at sport and hopelessly impractical. The child learned much later that it suffered from a disability classed as 'dyspraxia', a difficulty with coordination that might affect several things. This might be learning, handwriting, ball games, bike riding or social interaction. The thing is, I know what that was like, as I was that child! With me, it is ball games and bike riding that are the types of problem – I have a strong creative/imaginative drive and a strong academic leaning, though it takes me absolute ages to work out how to assemble an IKEA set of drawers! It was only in recent years that I heard about 'dyspraxia' and it was such a joy to wear a label. The power in that sort of word makes you part of a group and not alone. A burden lifts off your shoulders. Truth to tell, I still can't get on a bike and get very far without falling off. Maybe with grit and perseverance I could learn, but if I am honest, I don't want to. Childhood experiences and humiliations deflate you too much. I can drive a car, after all... that took ages and much determination, but that is another story.

The Word of God
The opening chapter of Genesis talks about God's word over and over again. 'And God said' recurs throughout the chapter, and after each 'word', something new comes into being. The phrase 'God said' occurs nine times.

The 'word' in the Scriptures is a part of God and his power. Words were not just empty or symbols, but expressions of power and purpose to be taken very seriously. God's word spoke creation into being and was powerful, achieving what it declared:

As the rain and the snow
come down from heaven,
    and do not return to it
without watering the earth
    and making it bud and flourish,
so that it yields seed for the sower and bread for the eater,
    so is my word that goes out from my mouth:
It will not return to me empty,
    but will accomplish what I desire
and achieve the purpose for which I sent it.

(Isaiah 55:10–11)

God spoke into his world once it was made; he did not leave it aloof and alone. He was intimately involved, sending prophets and teachers and revealing his word.

In the New Testament, this intimate, passionate involvement is brought to a fine, sharp point, focused par excellence in Jesus, 'the Word [become] flesh'.

Jesus is seen as God's Word in the Gospel of John.

In the beginning was the Word, and the Word was with God, and the Word was God. He was with God in the beginning.

Through him all things were made; without him nothing was made that has been made. In him was life, and that life was the light of men.   (John 1:1–4)

The evangelist goes on to say that the Word was made flesh:

> The Word became flesh and made his dwelling among us. We have seen his glory, the glory of the One and Only, who came from the Father, full of grace and truth.
>
> (John 1:14)

Jesus was the embodiment of God in creation. The creative power of the Word made flesh is attested in various places in the New Testament, extending out from the incarnation into the life of the believer. The Word can come into our spirits and make things new:

> Let the word of Christ dwell in you richly as you teach and admonish one another with all wisdom, and as you sing psalms, hymns and spiritual songs with gratitude in your hearts to God.   (Colossians 3:16)

> For God, who said, 'Let light shine out of darkness,' made his light shine in our hearts to give us the light of the knowledge of the glory of God in the face of Christ.
> But we have this treasure in jars of clay to show that this all-surpassing power is from God and not from us.
>
> (2 Corinthians 4:6–7)

> For you have been born again, not of perishable seed, but of imperishable, through the living and enduring word of God.   (1 Peter 1:23)

Reading through the above verses, I can think of Heather who started the Alpha course and after week one was so engrossed that she read the whole of Nicky Gumbel's companion book, *Questions of Life*. When she returned for the second week, she was lively and excited, declaring 'It's happened! I have given my life to Jesus and he has come in!' That was wonderful, but I was flabbergasted; that was not meant to happen until much later! Or I can think of Paul who went to hear a preacher after being pulled along by his girlfriend, felt challenged by the gospel and responded to an appeal to come forward. He knew that something different was in his life afterwards. There was a peace and a presence that could not be explained. The most beautiful miracle is the regeneration of the human spirit when we are brought back to God and new life comes into us.

The Seed

Gardens and Lives

'Mighty oaks from little acorns do grow'... Seeds are small, insignificant, but full of potential. Archaeologists found a cache of ancient seeds in one of the pyramids, nearly 3,000 years old. When they were brought out into the sunlight, planted and watered, they sprouted. Seeds are durable and ready to burst with life. My gardening skills are non-existent, but watch the efforts of the dedicated green-fingers who transform a desolate patch into a beautiful garden of delights. It takes time and patience, but it pays off. There is a stately home near to where I live and the old gardens are a pleasure to visit. There is a rich variety of colour, size, hardy perennials, summer blossoms and wild areas. It is tranquil, a place to chill out in the midst of craziness.

We can use 'seeds' as metaphors for the potential in human beings, all the skills and creativity that can be channelled and nurtured, and our care of children at home, in the nursery or the classroom.

The Righteous Seed

In the Old Testament, 'seed' is used to delineate the people of Israel, the righteous line, the chosen lineage that runs from Adam to the Messiah.

As curses are proclaimed on the first human beings after the fall, there is a prophetic word given about future hope and redemption:

> And I will put enmity
> between you and the woman,
> and between your offspring and hers;
>   he will crush your head,
> and you will strike his heel. (Genesis 3:15)

The offspring of the woman would redeem the human race. The serpent is a striking symbol of evil, of the devil, and was so in much of the religion of the ancient Near East. They strike without warning, slithering away, causing pain and death. They lived in the wild places, away from civilization. In the story of Gilgamesh from ancient Sumeria, the hero finds a magical plant that will give him eternal life. It is stolen away as he swims by a serpent. I don't like snakes, I will confess, and perhaps the Bible has given them a bad press. I know people who delight in them as pets and hug them and wrap them around their necks. I shudder at the thought. I can think of one young family – bless them – who insist on bringing their precious serpent to our annual Pet Service in church. When it comes up to the altar for a blessing, it is one beast that I do not touch!

I was once nagged into attending a snake charming show in a reptilarium in France. They had hired a charmer from Marrakesh and he blew his gourd to announce the start of the show. He pulled snakes this way and that, grabbing volunteers from the audience to have them on their heads, down their shirts and you name it. Let us just say that I perspired heavily! Personally, I don't like snakes. Have I made myself clear?

In Catholic tradition, the Virgin Mary is often shown crushing the serpent under her heel. This follows the Latin Vulgate Bible which translates the verse from Genesis as 'she will crush...' Thus, Catholic statues of Mary often have her stepping on the serpent. The Hebrew text actually is neutral 'it shall crush...' but the Greek translation, the Septuagint, translated this as 'he shall crush...' making it messianic. This has been followed by most English translations in recent times. Perhaps the Latin does not have the best translation, but an edifying message can be gleaned from this. It is not saying that Mary is the saviour. In fact, Mary here is seen as the second Eve whose obedience unravels Eve's disobedience by agreeing to the angel's message and becoming the mother of the saviour, or the doorway through which he steps into the world:

> 'I am the Lord's servant,' Mary answered. 'May it be to me as you have said.' Then the angel left her.   (Luke 1:38)

Mary's obedience is only of worth because she allows Jesus to be born.

The theme of the righteous or chosen seed continues in Genesis in the call of Abram:

The Lord had said to Abram, 'Leave your country, your people and your father's household and go to the land I will show you.

I will make you into a great nation
   and I will bless you;
I will make your name great,
   and you will be a blessing.
I will bless those who bless you,
   and whoever curses you I will curse;
and all peoples on earth
   will be blessed through you.   (Genesis 12:1–3)

The promised seed began to emerge with Isaac, the son of Abraham. Against all odds, when Sarah should have been past childbearing and had been barren, Isaac was born. His name, in Hebrew, means 'laughter', a laughter that would adorn the redeemed. From this lineage sprang the heroes of the Old Testament and, finally, Jesus himself. Paul speaks of the righteous seed thus:

The promises were spoken to Abraham and to his seed. The Scripture does not say 'and to seeds', meaning many people, but 'and to your seed', meaning one person, who is Christ.   (Galatians 3:16)

The seed is sometimes referred to as 'the seed of David', marking the royal descent and all the promised blessings made to that line:

Paul, a servant of Christ Jesus, called to be an apostle and set apart for the gospel of God – the gospel he promised beforehand through his prophets in the Holy Scriptures regarding his Son, who as to his human nature was a descendant of David, and who through the Spirit of holiness was declared with power to be the Son of God, by his resurrection from the dead: Jesus Christ our Lord.

(Romans 1:1–4)

The Ark

A Place of Safety

Think of the blessed relief when we have been in the thick of trouble and things calm down. We get out of a scrape, pay off a debt, and escape trouble. I remember a time, in my reckless youth, when I was hiking around the countryside with a friend. We decided to take a short cut down a slope towards a river. What we did not realize was that the slope we had embarked upon was far steeper than we thought. As we descended, it became clearer and clearer. Then I noticed that the foliage was giving way; the soil was loose, as though it had recently been dumped there. At this point I rested on a tree trunk that protruded. My friend ran down, seeing a sheer drop over the verge and narrowly missing some rocks. There was a splash, and he shouted to me. I could not move. Behind me was slurry and below me was more loose earth. I had no chance of gaining enough momentum to leap to safety. I was well and truly stuck. There was only one thing for it, he had to call for help. The fire brigade arrived and set up a line and a harness and they reeled me in. I felt a prize idiot but also very, very relieved and very, very safe.

Sometimes, we need to feel that we are in a place of spiritual safety. In all the religions of the world, there is a desire for peace with God and assurance of forgiveness. What they lack is that assurance. They are just left with hope. In Jesus, there is a place of safety.

Safe in the Ark

The story of Noah's ark prefigures salvation in Jesus. People are warned about the judgment to come and they are given an open invitation to enter the ark, but they refuse. Noah and his family are spared. They enter a place of safety, a place of salvation.

> The Lord then said to Noah, 'Go into the ark, you and your whole family, because I have found you righteous in this generation.' (Genesis 7:1)

In Jesus, there is peace. The first preaching of the apostle Peter urged people to flee coming judgment and to enter safety through Jesus:

> Repent and be baptised, every one of you, in the name of Jesus Christ for the forgiveness of your sins. And you will receive the gift of the Holy Spirit. (Acts 2:38)

Listen also to these words of hope from Ephesians 1:13:

> And you also were included in Christ when you heard the word of truth...

Paul uses the term 'in Christ' many times in his letter. We rest in and abide in Christ when we place our trust in him.

The Sacrifice

Something Costly

Giving something up can be a struggle, but a sacrifice is meant to be costly. We might go out of our way to comfort someone, or rush across the country to visit a sick relative in hospital. We might give some money and forgo a holiday or an upgrade on a TV. If it is a worthy cause, there will be a sense of peace, relief and fulfilment after the struggle. Any true sacrifice comes from a willing heart.

The shedding of blood is seen as sacred in various traditional cultures. There is controversy over the slaying of a bull in an African diocese as I write, for example. This is planned as a part of the festivities for the founding of that diocese. Locals argue that this is their culture and a way of showing that it is something serious; outsiders wonder and criticize the act as being too pagan.

The ancient Near East made binding covenants between different parties by offering sacrifices, and blood was shed to mark the seriousness of the agreements and the oaths. God had made a covenant with Abraham (see Genesis 15) to confirm the promise of blessing to all nations through his offspring. Sacrifices could also be made in the worship of these ancient lands to appease the deity, to honour the deity by offering something costly, and to atone for sins.

The Sacrifice of Isaac
Sadly, some ancient tribes were so under fear of the gods that they practised child sacrifice, offering the firstborn child. It sounds ghastly, and it was. None of Abraham's ancestors are known to have used such a vile form of offering, but Abraham felt challenged to do so. Remember that he had lived among pagan neighbours in Ur of the Chaldeans and had travelled along the fertile crescent area of the Tigris and Euphrates rivers. He would have been exposed to many such weird cultic practices.

The Genesis story suggests that this was a test and, thankfully, God spared Isaac at the last moment, providing the ram that was caught in the thicket. The social background of this event helps us to realize how God could have used such a test. Today it would be cruel and barbarically unthinkable.

> But the angel of the Lord called out to him from heaven, 'Abraham! Abraham!'
>
> 'Here I am,' he replied.
>
> 'Do not lay a hand on the boy,' he said. 'Do not do anything to him. Now I know that you fear God, because you have not withheld from me your son, your only son.'
>
> Abraham looked up and there in a thicket he saw a ram caught by its horns. He went over and took the ram and sacrificed it as a burnt offering instead of his son. So Abraham called that place The Lord Will Provide. And to this day it is said, 'On the mountain of the Lord it will be provided.'
>
> The angel of the Lord called to Abraham from heaven a second time and said, 'I swear by myself, declares the Lord, that because you have done this and have not withheld your son, your only son, I will surely bless you and make your descendants as numerous as the stars in the sky and as the sand on the seashore. Your descendants will take possession of the cities of their enemies, and through your offspring all nations on earth will be blessed, because you have obeyed me.'
>
> (Genesis 22:11–18)

The lamb offered in sacrifice prefigured Jesus as the Lamb of God, and the offering of Abraham's precious and only son prefigured the offering of Jesus on the cross. There pain wracked the heart of God as the Son was given up by the Father and the Holy Spirit hovered, waiting until the offering was over.

What, then, shall we say in response to this? If God is for us, who can be against us? He who did not spare his own Son, but gave him up for us all how will he not also, along with him, graciously give us all things?

(Romans 8:32–33)

That 'giving up' was a heart cry of God throughout all eternity. Abraham had struggled and believed for Isaac, the son of the promise, the righteous seed of the line of blessing. To offer him in sacrifice would have been unthinkable as a father and doubly unthinkable as a prophet. Perhaps be believed that the power of God would raise Isaac up as the promise was upon him (and this is suggested in Hebrews 11:19). God spared him, but when he entered his creation himself, he did not spare himself, but drank the bitter dregs of the cup of suffering.

Christian Sacrifice

Sometimes there is a call, a challenge to offer up the very thing that we have believed for, maybe a sense of vocation as a missionary marries and raises a family, or an artist leaves their craft for a time to work in some other way for God. Maybe these old callings never come back and fulfilment and service are found in the new roles. The old ways have been tests and preparations. Or, they do return, refined and strengthened, as opportunities arise and circumstances change. Priorities are different, people have learned to trust more and maturity has developed. I recall the example of a musician called Derek who loved to play the double bass. After his conversion he felt challenged to give this up – and I must stress how unusual this call to abandon talent tends to be – and he did so after quite a struggle. In fact, as an act of triumph and declaration, he smashed his instrument to bits! In later months, someone bought him a new double bass, moved by God to do so. Derek had been tried and tested, proven and newly commissioned.

On a more serious front, think of the missionaries who went into Ecuador's rainforest led by Jim Elliott. He and four other young men made contact with the Aucas, a primitive tribe who would not think twice to kill. The men were murdered, soon after setting up a base and believing that they had responded to God's call. Their martyrdom opened the gate for blessing, though, as the widows returned, forgave the tribe and worked patiently with them. Many conversions followed. Their killers admitted that they had heard angelic singing in the air after they had shed the blood of the innocent. Their blood was the seed of the church.

The Ruler

Jesus is the Lamb and the place of salvation in Genesis, but he is also authority in the Word and in the crown. He is the Messiah to come.

Towards the end of Genesis there is a remarkable prophecy given by Jacob over one of his sons, Judah. In the near east, fathers would give their blessing to their sons before they died. This was not only a great honour, but it gave permission to build for the future, a security and a sense of being cherished and released into life.

You are a lion's cub, O Judah;
    you return from the prey, my son.
Like a lion he crouches and lies down,
    like a lioness who dares to rouse him?

The sceptre will not depart from Judah,
    nor the ruler's staff from between his feet,
until he comes to whom it belongs
    and the obedience of the nations is his.
He will tether his donkey to a vine,
    his colt to the choicest branch;
he will wash his garments in wine,
    his robes in the blood of grapes.
His eyes will be darker than wine,
    his teeth whiter than milk.   (Genesis 49:9–12)

Judah was to be the royal tribe from whence the future kings would come from David through to Jesus, the King of kings. Jesus is known as the 'Lion of Judah'. The sceptre, the rule, would be placed into the hands of one who is to come until all the nations bow before him.

The reference to washing his clothes in wine and his robes in the blood of grapes suggests the passion and the blood shed on the cross to redeem us. Jesus is the Servant King who stooped low in the manger and went to the cross for us.

It should be noted that the other Jewish tribes were defeated, scattered and lost; only Judah remained and the name passed over to the race and faith – 'Jews' and 'Judaism' come from 'Judah'.

This idea of 'one who is to come' springs up from time to time in the early sections of the Old Testament, without any clear detail – as in Balaam's prophecy in Numbers 24:17–19 for example. Again, one will come from Judah to rule. Another king motif is found in the figure of the ancient king of Salem, Melchizedek (Genesis 14:18–24). Melchizedek blesses Abraham by God Most High (the ancient name *El Elyon*). The king's name means 'King of

Righteousness' and Salem means 'peace', the ancient name for Jerusalem, the centre of the later kingdom of Judah and the royal city of David and the Messiah. We know nothing about Melchizedek. He suddenly appears in the narrative, prompting the author of Hebrews in the New Testament to read things into this passage. Melchizedek becomes a type of Christ and the absence of any detail about his background becomes a 'happy coincidence' that suggests, playfully, the eternal nature of the Son before and after the incarnation (see Hebrews 7:1–3). He was probably a figure creating great speculation in the time of Jesus. In the Dead Sea Scrolls, he is a heavenly figure who will help Israel. Melchizedek will surface when we look at the Psalms, too, and aspects of the kingly ritual from his day probably lived on in David's Jerusalem. It too could speak of Jesus as we shall see.

Tail-ending – Ladders and Angels

Genesis has other details that some see as pointing to Jesus, such as the vision of Jacob's ladder (Genesis 28:12–19) when Jacob slept and dreamed of a ladder connecting heaven and earth with the angels ascending and descending. Jesus refers to this in John 1:51 when he tells Nathaniel:

> ...you shall see heaven open, and the angels of God ascending and descending on the Son of Man.

Jesus himself is the bridge between heaven and earth, through the incarnation.

One final pointer is the figure of the Angel of the Lord who appears to Hagar in the wilderness (see Genesis

16:7–14). There are angels, archangels and 'the Angel of the Lord'. The latter almost seems to be a representation of the Lord, a manifestation somehow, for he speaks with God's voice and authority (thus verse 10, 'I will so increase your descendants that they will be too numerous to count'). This figure pops up in other books and can be seen as the pre-existent Son.

This chapter has been a long haul through the first book of the Bible, for this is rich and fertile ground. We should expect all the major themes of Scripture to be present or hinted at here, at least in embryonic form.

PRAYER

Father, I thank you that your word is powerful and creative, calling things into being that are not. I thank you that you can speak into my life and make me new. I thank you that I am born of the righteous seed, a co-heir with Christ, safe and saved in him. I thank you for his death on the cross, a love stronger than death that gave his all for me and rose again triumphant. Amen.

MEMORY VERSE

And I will put enmity
between you and the woman,
    and between your offspring and hers;
he will crush your head,
    and you will strike his heel. (Genesis 3:15)

Jesus in Exodus

The book of Exodus is about coming out of bondage, being set free. Moses was called to lead the Hebrews out of slavery in Egypt. This is a book that speaks of redemption and sacrifice.

The key types of Jesus in Exodus are

- The Passover lamb
- Passing through the sea
- The bitter lake
- The bread and water of life
- The tabernacle
- The high priest

Life for a Life

He felt a hand about to shove him back. The SS guard looked angrily at the Franciscan friar who had stepped forward and bowed his head before him. What did he want?

The friar spoke. He wanted to offer his life in place of that of a married man.

Earlier, three prisoners had escaped from Auschwitz and the guards ordered executions in retaliation. Ten men were selected. They were to be sent to the Bunker, a series of underground cells where they would be starved to death. One of the men was Franciszek Gajowniczek. He sighed, 'Oh, my wife, my poor children... I shall never see them again.'

The guard was bemused but accepted the exchange. Father Maximilian Kolbe stepped into the line of condemned men. They said that he comforted the dying men for days, singing hymns and leading prayers. He was the last to die, with the name of Jesus on his lips.

Franciszek Gajowniczek survived the war and was present as an old man in St Peter's Square when Pope John Paul II declared that Father Maximilian was a saint of the Catholic Church. This was on 10 October 1982. Thus Father Maximilian had fulfilled the words of Jesus, 'Greater love has no-one than this, that he lay down his life for his friends' (John 15:13).[1]

Another time, another place. In Lebanon in the 1990s, the Dutch evangelist Brother Andrew (of *God's Smuggler* fame) had arranged a meeting with Ayatollah Fadlallah. He hoped to broker a deal to release some hostages, particularly a Christian whom he had heard was unwell. They were courteous to each other, shared coffee, verses from the Bible and discussed Christianity. Then Brother Andrew made his offer. He wanted to exchange himself for the hostage. A life for a life. His affairs were in order, his children grown up. The Ayatollah looked at him as if he were mad. After a few moments he whispered, 'How can you say that?'

Brother Andrew went on to explain about the spirit of Christ and the way he died on a cross to set us all free. The Ayatollah was astounded. He had never heard Christianity so expressed or lived out. Brother Andrew's request was

---

1. Antonio Ricciardi, *Saint Maximilian Kolbe*, Boston: Pauline Books & Media.

refused, but he was seen as a man of honour and holiness from then on by the Ayatollah's followers.[2]

The Passover Lamb

Jesus' death to liberate and forgive is foreshadowed superbly in Exodus. This is seen first of all in the type of the Passover lamb. The Passover festival commemorates the time when the Hebrews were protected from the destroying angel that came upon Egypt. They were spared so long as they remained in their houses and sacrificed a lamb. The blood was daubed on the door lintels and the lamb was eaten inside after being roasted. The Lord told Moses: '...when I see the blood, I will pass over you' (Exodus 12:13).

Jesus is called the Lamb of God by John the Baptist: 'Look, the Lamb of God, who takes away the sin of the world!' (John 1:29).

Paul equates Jesus with the Passover sacrifice: 'For Christ, our Passover lamb, has been sacrificed' (1 Corinthians 5:7).

This is an aversion sacrifice, to be technical. The shed blood of the offering averts the wrath of God which is justly deserved. More needs to be said about the types of the different Hebrew sacrifices in the Torah to draw out the multifarious mystery of the atonement.

Note, too, that the lamb was to be consumed within the house. Both rituals were necessary; covering and eating. In this we can see a type of receiving the life of Christ,

---

2 Brother Andrew with Al Janssen, *Light Force*, Grand Rapids, MI: Chosen Books, 2004.

though the Holy Spirit, within the believer as well as a confession of faith in the blood of the cross.

Passing Through the Sea

After a wind blew all night, Moses led the Hebrews to safety through the waters of the Yam Suph. The Hebrew term means, literally, 'Sea of Reeds' rather than 'Red Sea' and would have been a lake or an inlet of the Nile delta. Whatever, wherever exactly it was, they passed through. The New Testament sees this as a type of baptism:

> For I do not want you to be ignorant of the fact, brothers, that our forefathers were all under the cloud and that they passed through the sea. They were all baptised into Moses in the cloud and in the sea.　　(1 Corinthians 10:1–2)

Paul uses the cloud that guided the Hebrews by day as a symbol of covering moisture here, interestingly. They were covered by this and also went through the waters. Just so, the believer today is covered by the sacrifice of Christ and passes through repentance and cleansing in baptism.

The Bitter Lake

Exodus 14:22–27 tells the story of the Hebrews arriving at the waters of Marah, a word that means 'bitter', for they were undrinkable. The people complained to Moses and he prayed. God told him to take a specific piece of wood, which he threw into the waters, making them sweet. What that wood was we do not know; whether this was a supernatural miracle or a result of God's providence through chemicals in that wood, we cannot tell. This incident is seen as a type of the cross. When the cross is brought to our human pride, hurt and bitterness, there is a healing, a change. Converted hearts find their feelings change. Barriers come down. The heart of stone can become a heart of flesh. I recall a Hungarian couple singing a song, 'Jesus, Thy Cross is Sweet to Me', many years ago. I cannot remember the rest of the words, but they sang it as a praise song, honouring all the changes that had been worked by grace in their lives.

The cross can deal with division and bitterness between people. I think of a time when I was at loggerheads with a fellow believer whom I had shared a flat with for a time. Relationships were strained and we both talked with a mediator. The amazing thing was that we were both saying very similar things about each other – maybe we can't stand the weaknesses in others that we know are in ourselves. After coming together and bringing this before the Lord, wisely avoiding any circular arguments and accusations, the atmosphere broke. Now, I wouldn't say that we ever became bosom buddies, but a wall had come down and grace flowed. The power of the Holy Spirit can mend things that we can never put right in our own strength. Or, again, I recall a documentary that showed two inmates in Northern Ireland who were both serving time for belonging to paramilitary organisations. One was a Catholic and one a Protestant. They had met the Lord in prison, been genuinely born anew, washed clean by the blood of the cross, and now were as one. They had a love for each other and forgave each other.

> Therefore, if anyone is in Christ, he is a new creation; the old has gone, the new has come!   (2 Corinthians 5:17)

The Bread and Water of Life

Food and drink is a basic human necessity, a great social leveller and one that, once shared, binds groups together in human fellowship. In the stories in Exodus, we see God's care and provision for the Hebrews in the desert in the heavenly manna and the water from the rock. This is chronicled in Exodus 16 and 17. The Lord says: 'I will rain down bread from heaven for you' (Exodus 16:4) and 'Strike the rock, and water will come out of it for the people to drink' (Exodus 17:6).

Being put in the middle of nowhere with little to eat is no laughing matter. There can be a profound humility, sense of sharing and appreciation in such circumstances. I remember sitting with some people on a hillside in the mist. The party had to stop until it cleared. Sandwiches had been consumed much earlier. All that anyone had left was a pack of compressed, dried bananas. They look revolting, all shrivelled, flat and brown. In fact, they tasted sublime in those circumstances, sweet and energy enhancing, as they were carefully split up and shared around.

The manna was sweet as honey to the taste. These thin, white flakes that covered the ground might have been the secretions of desert insects according to the scholars; we do not know. They were seen as the miraculous provision of God however they were provided, and they contained the energy and nutrition needed.

Jesus compared his flesh to the manna in John's Gospel: 'For the bread of God is he who comes down from heaven and gives life to the world' (John 6:33).

Water quenches thirst, cools and gives life. Think of the classic scene in the movie *Ice Cold in Alex* where the heroes find their way across the desert and order a beer from a bar. They sit and look at it for a moment, entranced, delighted, and then they gulp it down.

The water from the rock, probably a spring that flowed beneath layers of limestone rock, spoke of blessing and provision. Moses was guided to the very spot where he could allow this to break through. In the New Testament, Paul calls the rock 'Christ':

> They all ate the same spiritual food and drank the same spiritual drink; for they drank from the spiritual rock that accompanied them, and that rock was Christ.
>
> (1 Corinthians 10:3–4)

Gushing water suggests other images in the Gospels, too, such as Jesus as 'living water': 'Indeed, the water I give him will become in him a spring of water welling up to eternal life' (John 4:14).

Eating and drinking suggests holy communion, too. This is inescapable, for Jesus gave us a sacred meal at the heart of our worship, however we understand this. Many are the theologies, the mysteries and the delights. At the heart of all beliefs is the encounter with the risen Lord, the sharing in his life and his Spirit, as well as the proclamation through word and symbol of his saving death. There is food for the soul as well as the body and we are in the presence of the living Lord. It is not just about a memory, nostalgically expressed, but rejoicing in a present awareness. This was expressed so clearly by Tony Melendez, a young man born without arms. He was one of the Thalidomide babies born in the 1960s with various deformities. Tony became adept at picking things up with his feet and he became an accomplished guitar player by using his toes. He has since released albums and written his autobiography. Tony was drawn into faith by the example of an energetic young priest. When he received communion, he did not pretend to know how it worked or in what sense Jesus was present, he just knew that he was. His touch, his grace and his life were all that mattered.

The Tabernacle

We all need a sense of place. There are some places that are special to us. There might be memories associated, such as a sporting achievement or a romance. The site of car fatalities will engender emotion for years, as flowers are left by the roadside. Sometimes we seek out a peaceful place where we can be alone and think – on top of the English South Downs, perhaps, near to where I live now. A few years ago, I lived near an extensive forest and I would weave my way through the pathways until I came across an isolated, hidden pond. There was a solitary bench, and I would sit and listen, watching a leaf fall.

Sacred places are about encounter with the living God. There are places, today, where pilgrims flock. There has been great blessing there – maybe a tomb of a saint or the site of one of Jesus' miracles. A visitor to the tomb of the prophet Ezekiel in Iraq reported that the sense of holiness was palpable. Yes, God is everywhere, but there can be special places that move and inspire. I visited the tiny French village of Ars recently where a saintly Curé, Jeanne Marie Vianney, was parish priest in the early nineteenth century. His tomb stands in the old church and it is a place of pilgrimage. You can feel the prayer. The place is heavy with it.

Some places are just prayed in, prayer soaked, and

carry a sense of God and a touch of blessing. The Hebrews had the tabernacle in the wilderness. Yet, there is a crucial difference. Many places can be blessed and peaceful. The tabernacle was a specially designated meeting place, a holy zone where God could be approached, and only here. This was a provision made because of the sinfulness of humanity. Jesus has removed the need for such a location. We have access to the Father through him anywhere, at any time and in any place. Nowhere is special in this sense, though some places do carry associations with holiness and prayerfulness.

Exodus 36–40 details the design and the layout. A courtyard of white sheets of linen surrounded the tabernacle. A gateway of coloured cloth allowed you to enter the courtyard. The colours were blue, purple, scarlet and fine linen.

In front of the tabernacle was a sacrificial altar and a large laver, or bowl, behind this for the priests to wash in. The same three-coloured curtain covered the entrance to the tabernacle. This would have looked unimpressive from the outside, as it was covered with badgers' skins. It would have looked like a chieftains' hut in an encampment, rough and ragged. It was clearly a holy place as it was in the white courtyard, but once entering, it was like going through the wardrobe and finding the wonders of Narnia. Inside were colours and embroidered cherubim. There were gold poles and rings, and furniture. There were clouds of perfumed incense. Before a second curtain, the veil that separated the Holy Place from sight, there were the golden lampstand signifying the presence of God; the altar of incense signifying worship and intercession; and the table of the bread of the presence. Fresh loaves were brought before the Lord each day. Here you sensed the holy, light, presence, offering, life.

Behind the veil was the Holy Place, and in here was the ark of the covenant, a gold covered chest that could have poles attached so that it could be carried. On its lid were two angels positioned so that the tips of their wings touched, forming a canopy. All glittering gold. The area above the lid and beneath the wings was the mercy seat, the place where the high priest would come once a year and sprinkle the sacrificial blood. There he would make atonement for the sins of the people and ask for mercy. The glory of God hovered, the Shekinah, above the mercy seat. The word for the lid of the ark was the place of 'covering' or 'atonement'. Here atonement was made by offering shed blood. This spoke of the holiness of God and the seriousness of sin. Debates rage about how the Hebrew term should be translated. *Kapparah* or *kapar* means to cover or to wipe clean. In Greek it is *ilaserion* which can convey the sense of expiation or propitiation. The former speaks of clearing away or covering up. The latter speaks also of averting wrath or seeing justice done. Perhaps both senses need to be affirmed. God in his mercy stoops low and gives a way of covering sin, cleansing the sinner and making atonement. In his justice, he sees the principle of 'a life for a life', blood shed to appease and rectify. There can be some ugly theologies of a wrathful God and this must always be tempered by his mercy. The Torah gives a strong sense of the holiness of God and the destructive barrier of sin. Atonement is a serious business.

What do these things tell us of Jesus?
On the outside, Jesus was a just a man, not a Superman or a god but flesh and blood that could feel hunger and pain. Isaiah spoke of him thus: 'He had no beauty or majesty to

attract us to him, nothing in his appearance that we should desire him' (Isaiah 53:2).

On the inside, there was the hidden majesty of God, the fullness of God: 'And God placed all things under his feet and appointed him to be head over everything for the church, which is his body, the fulness of him who fills everything every way' (Ephesians 1:22–23).

In the prologue to John's Gospel, Jesus is identified with the tabernacle: 'The Word became flesh and made his dwelling among us' (John 1:14).

The Greek here means 'tabernacled' or 'made his tent' among us. Later in that Gospel, Jesus points to the stones of the Temple and says: 'Destroy this temple, and I will raise it again in three days' (John 2:19). The evangelist adds the comment: 'But the temple he had spoken of was his body' (John 2:21).

Another detail about the tabernacle that should be noted is that there were rams' skins dyed red under the badger skins. The symbol of a blood covering separated the mundane from the holy. It is under the blood that we have access to the Lord.

We can approach the presence of the living God through the altar of sacrifice, the washing, and enter into his presence in worship and intercession. Thus through the blood of Christ, through being washed by this and his Word, through the waters of baptism we are brought into the light and there we can offer praises and prayers: 'For God, who said, "Let light shine out of darkness", made his light shine in our hearts to give us the light of the knowledge of the glory of God in the face of Christ' (2 Corinthians 4:6).

Looking again at the furnishings in the outer part of the tabernacle, Jesus is the light of the world, the high priest who makes intercession for us, and the Bread of Life.

When we move into the Holy Place, we see the culmination of Christ's sacrifice. The epistle to the Hebrews draws out all the symbolism and preaches Jesus wonderfully. The high priest went inside once a year on the Day of Atonement (Yom Kippur) and presented the blood. Jesus passed into heaven, directly into the presence of God. This is the perfect, real Holy Place that the tabernacle copied symbolically. There he presented his blood once for all, and the wounds that he still bears, voluntarily, are an eternal testimony to that offering.

> But now he has appeared once for all at the end of the ages to do away with sin by the sacrifice of himself... Christ was sacrificed once to take away the sins of many people; and he will appear a second time, not to bear sin, but to bring salvation to those who are waiting for him.
>
> (Hebrews 9:26b, 28)

Deep in the heart of the New Testament theology of the cross is a sense of propitiation. It sounds harsh and judicial perhaps today, but it is there, deeply embedded in the tradition. It is there for a purpose, for sin is serious and redemption is costly: 'Since we have now been justified by his blood, how much more shall we be saved from God's wrath through him' (Romans 5:9).

When we survey the other types of sacrifices in the Torah, other angles and nuances will appear about the cross. Propitiation and aversion were not the only things going on, but they were there. Understood rightly, propitiation language is love language, for when sinful humanity could not atone for their sins, God, holy and righteous, but rich in mercy, stooped low and took flesh, taking the punishment, offering the sacrifice himself. It was an act of love from start to finish. The shadowy, imperfect provision of the Old Testament cult was also an act of mercy for the Jews.

As ours is a Trinitarian faith, then the Father and the Son cannot be totally separated. They are involved one in another, inescapably. We do not and cannot understand the pain in God's heart when Jesus was on the cross. Paul tells us that the Father had to abandon the Son: 'He who did not spare his own Son, but gave him up for us all' (Romans 8:32), and that would have been a searing pain in any father's heart. In the mystery of the Trinity, they are involved in each other and cannot be totally separated out. When it is suggested that propitiation theology is a form of divine child abuse, this is most offensive and treats Jesus as a separate deity, rather like the ancient heresy of Arianism. Orthodox Christianity cannot pull apart the Persons; what happens to one intimately affects the others.

Propitiation language is love language. The illustration is often used of a judge stepping into the dock himself to take the rap. That is the awesome mystery of the cross. God stepped into his creation to bear the sin of the world and only love made him do it. The sacrificial imagery in Exodus reminds us of the depth of darkness that some people fall into. Think of victims of the Rwanda massacre facing their enemies and seeking to forgive. Not only has Jesus shown amazing love, but he has faced the darkness, carried it, stared it in the face, owned it, defeated it and can take us beyond it. That is power unlike any other. Truth to tell, people sometimes can be plain evil, but there is redemption.

'In Christ'

Paul often uses the expression to be 'in Christ', secure, located, rooted, safe. Through confession of faith, repentance and baptism, the believer is 'in Christ', a member of his Body. The symbolism of the veil and the Holy Place speaks of this entrance and incorporation. Once through the curtain, we stand within the Holy Place. Jesus himself is the 'gate' or the 'door' (see John 10:7–9). Hebrews speaks of the boldness we can now have to approach the throne of grace, through the blood of Christ. The veil has been torn open and we have free access if we are in Christ:

> Therefore, brothers, since we have the confidence to enter the Most Holy Place by the blood of Jesus, by a new and living way opened for us through the curtain, that is, his body... let us draw near to God with a sincere heart in full assurance of faith...
> (Hebrews 10:19, 22)

Matthew's Gospel relates that the veil was torn in two in the Holy Place when Jesus died (see Matthew 27:51).

The High Priest

Canon Andrew White is based in Baghdad as an Anglican priest running the church of St George, and helping in various peace and reconciliation work. He heads up the Foundation for Reconciliation in the Middle East.

He tells many amazing and daring stories of rushing around the country and hovering in helicopters that are constantly shot at. He is admired by many Iraqis and by the Muslim clerics as a devout, sincere and trustworthy man. He relates the story of how he was asked by the various Muslim leaders to take on the position of Head of

Islamic Affairs after the fall of Saddam Hussein. He was the only person they trusted to do the job, to navigate between interests and different groups. A Christian priest was thus approached! He went to ask the Archbishop of Canterbury who said 'No', but he returned, refused the title, and did the essentials of the job anyway. His sensitivity does not compromise the gospel, and he and his team pray each day for protection and for miracles. Once, as the Iraqis were approaching the end of Ramadan and needed meat for the final festival, he was approached. He promised to do what he could. An American walked into his office and said, 'You guys need any meat?' Andrew asked if it was *halal*, suitable for Muslims to eat. It was; and a container full of suitable meat was delivered for their festival. This not only speaks of the provision and mercy of God, but of the power of the trusted go-between. Such a person is indispensable.

Exodus 39 describes the garments of the high priest and various priests, the go-betweens for the Hebrews. Aaron wore the words, 'Holy to the Lord' on his forehead and he wore a sacred garment on his shoulders and breast, bearing the names of the tribes of Israel. Jesus, according to Hebrews, is our high priest, who intercedes for the people. He is anointed with the Holy Spirit, he carries the people in his heart and on his shoulders, like the good shepherd who carried back the lost sheep.

> Therefore, since we have a great high priest who has gone into the heavens, Jesus the Son of God, let us hold firmly to the faith we profess. For we do not have a high priest who is unable to sympathise with our weaknesses, but we have one who has been tempted in every way, just as we are – yet was without sin. Let us then approach the throne

of grace with confidence, so that we may receive mercy and find grace to help us in our time of need.

(Hebrews 4:14–16)

PRAYER

Father, I thank you that I am saved by the blood of the Lamb. I am safe under his protection and I can pass through the waters of death, freed from the bondage of sin and the devil. I thank you that you can change my heart and remove its bitterness through the cross. I thank you that you feed me with the Bread of Life and nurture me with the water of the Spirit. I thank you that I can approach your presence boldly, coming into the Holy Place through the blood of Jesus, my great and abiding high priest. Amen.

MEMORY VERSE

'When I see the blood, I will pass over you.'

(Exodus 12:13)

Jesus in Leviticus

The book of Leviticus is not about the stories of Moses and the Hebrews wandering in the wilderness, though it is set in this time and originates from it. It is about the way of holiness. It is full of laws and rituals, ethics and procedures to live a holy life before the Lord. Some of these seem curious and dated to modern readers now, but they were highly relevant to a tribe living in desert conditions, and much abiding wisdom can be found in these ancient words. This is the old covenant, of course, and Jesus has fulfilled these laws. The ritual Law is set aside as a shadow of things to come (see Hebrews 10:1) but the ethical Law abides for ever.

Leviticus speaks of Jesus in the following ways:

- The sin offerings
- Ritual for cleansing a leper
- The scapegoat and the Day of Atonement

The Sin Offerings

How would you preach the cross to the following people?

- A member of an African tribe where primal, polytheistic religious beliefs are practised. A burning question in their minds will be 'What sort of sacrifice do the gods require from me?'

- A guilt-ridden person who has committed adultery and destroyed their marriage, or a convicted criminal who feels that if there is a God then he must hate him?
- Members of a family or racial groups where there is tension and hatred, violence even, between them.
- A sceptic who feels that Christians are hypocrites or wanting a crutch to lean on.

If we look at the various sacrificial offerings listed in Leviticus 1–5 they touch those needs and questions.

The Whole Burnt Offering

Chapter 1 gives instructions for an offering where the animal carcass is burnt up and no one eats any of it. The shed blood is sprinkled over the altar in the tabernacle courtyard first, but then the whole thing is offered up. The idea is that this is a total offering, a sweet perfume to the Lord, a gift with no strings attached. 'It is a burnt offering, an offering made by fire, an aroma pleasing to the Lord' (Leviticus 1:9).

This is a worship offering rather than an atonement offering though shed blood is sprinkled to stress that sinners approach God through the blood.

Thinking of our list of people above, this might give an angle for the sceptic. In Jesus we see one who gave himself completely to the Father's will (see Matthew 26:39), who went to the cross willingly for us, even though he could have called upon a legion of angels to save him from that fate. Greater love has no man. As Paul put it: 'You see, just at the right time, when we were still powerless, Christ died for the ungodly. Very rarely will anyone die for a righteous man, though for a good man someone might possibly dare to die. But God demonstrates his love for us in this: While we were still sinners, Christ died for us' (Romans 5:6–8).

In Ephesians, he picks up the theme of the sweet offering: '... live a life of love, just as Christ loved us and gave himself up for us as a fragrant offering and sacrifice to God' (Ephesians 5:2).

This is the foundation of our faith, a man who gave himself totally for us even when we despised him. This is the force that drove Father Maximilian to give his life for another in Auschwitz, as detailed in the last chapter. This powerful act of love, of service, of worship and abandonment is striking and converting.

The Fellowship Offering

An animal is slaughtered, its blood sprinkled, and some of the meat is eaten by all – not just the priests – and shared out. This is a fellowship offering in thanksgiving for a clan or family group. They make peace and affirm their support for one another.

Jesus gave himself to make peace between humanity and God. In Ephesians we read: 'But now in Christ Jesus you who were once far away have been brought near through the blood of Christ. For he himself is our peace, who has made the two one and has destroyed the barrier, the dividing wall of hostility' (Ephesians 2:13–14).

Jesus is a peacemaker and reconciler, and this is the angle, the message for a people divided. One image of how Jesus saves on the cross is to imagine two people with Jesus in the middle. He holds their hands and joins them together. One represents God, and the other humanity. By extension, we can see that his reconciliation has power and effect between people, too. There is a principle that once God and humanity were joined in the incarnation, we find God in humanity and not just beyond. He cares about peace and about broken and damaged relationships.

The Sin Offering

Leviticus 4–5 tables various sin offerings that are atoning in purpose. Bulls are used for intentional sins of individuals or the people. Goats are used for unintentional sin – to cover any eventualities, even if they never realize that they have sinned. Rams were used for guilt offerings, for times when the Hebrews sinned unintentionally, but later realized it, by mishandling any holy items in the tabernacle or religious system that Moses had given them.

These offerings were fulfilled by Jesus who offered himself for sin once and for all, making propitation and justifying us through his blood:

> When Christ came as high priest of the good things that are already here, he went through the greater and more perfect tabernacle that is not man-made, that is to say, not a part of this creation. He did not enter by means of the blood of goats and calves; but he entered the Most Holy Place once for all by his own blood, having obtained eternal redemption. (Hebrews 9:11–12)

This speaks to the guilt ridden who know that they have committed sin, that they have acted evilly. They know that they deserve judgment and wrath, but the mercy of God flows through the cross. Jesus has been there for them and has taken that wrath upon himself and into himself. That is liberation.

For the polytheist, worrying about the right sacrifice to offer, they are stopped in their tracks by the sacrifice of Christ. His once for all, total offering liberates from the need to constantly offer and worry about being accepted.

The above types of offering have demonstrated different angles on the meaning of the cross. Propitiatory atonement, total worship and an example of love unto death and a desire to make peace and reconcile. The mystery of the cross is many-faceted. There are other models and ideas, too, when you search the Scriptures and Christian tradition.

The Grain Offering

A further type of offering, found in Leviticus 2, is that of grain, offered in worship and thanksgiving, and not in atonement. If we look at the details of how this was to be prepared in verse 16, the grain is crushed, mixed with oil and incense and burned. Jesus was crushed, his body beaten beyond recognition: 'But he was pierced for our transgressions, he was crushed for our iniquities; the punishment that brought us peace was upon him, and by his wounds we are healed' (Isaiah 53:5).

The oil represents the Holy Spirit who was poured out upon Jesus and who was sent upon the believer after his death and resurrection: 'Exalted to the right hand of God, he has received from the Father the promised Holy Spirit and has poured out what you now see and hear' (Acts 2:33).

The incense is the sweet fragrance of his sacrifice and his interceding power for us.

Strange Fire!

There is a curious story in Leviticus 10:1–2 where Nadab and Abihu offer 'strange fire' (KJV) before the Lord and are judged. This means that offered incense that was not burned on coals from the altar of sacrifice. The incense had to touch that fire, had to touch that which was set apart to the Lord and had been sprinkled with the blood. Only worship through that was acceptable to God. Our worship today is acceptable to the Father when it is through Christ and his atoning sacrifice: 'you also, like living stones, are being built into a spiritual house to be a holy priesthood, offering spiritual sacrifices acceptable to God through Jesus Christ' (1 Peter 2:5).

There is a salutary warning here about interfaith worship. It is one thing to have dialogue, encounter groups and social programmes that share common human and spiritual values, but to worship God together is problematic. Other faiths are outside the covenant with the Lord and are very open to deception and corruption. There might be things that are good and true within them, but there are some teachings and rituals that are diametrically opposed to the Scriptures. Reincarnation cannot be squared with resurrection, for example, and Muhammad as the last prophet cannot be reconciled with Jesus as Lord. To try to pretend such differences are not real and substantial is to make a watery soup of the faiths and to deny them their individual integrities. It is also to compromise the uniqueness of Jesus and his Lordship. Holy fire must not be mixed with strange fire.

Ritual for Cleansing a Leper

Some of the Old Testament cleansing rituals seem very exotic to modern readers. The ritual for the cleansing of a leper in Leviticus 13 and 14 is one such example. Lepers were ritually unclean and had to stay outside the camp. If a leper was cured, then two sparrows were taken, brought outside the camp with the leper, and one was sacrificed. The leper was sprinkled with its blood and then the other was released into the air, to fly free.

Some see in this various symbols of Jesus. There is the cleansing by the blood and the fact that the sacrifice takes place outside the camp – a feature of the crucifixion as Jesus was taken to Mount Calvary outside the city of Jerusalem. The setting free of one bird is suggestive of the resurrection.

The Scapegoat and the Day of Atonement

Social anthropologists see a pattern, a dynamic in scapegoat episodes. A scapegoat is an animal or a person upon whom the blame is laid for some ill. They are named, declared guilty and driven outside the city. They are sent out never to return, taking the fear, anger and frustration with them. They go out to die in the wilderness. The ancient Greeks would scapegoat the socially undesirables – the disabled or the diseased or the criminals – sending them out in a time of crisis. They would be paraded around the city walls and cursed, put to death outside or driven away. These people became *pharmakoi*, ways of healing a pestilence on the city. In today's terms, when a social group decides to scapegoat someone, or another group, then all blame is poured onto their heads irrationally. They collect the dirt, get their characters defamed and lies spread about them. Hitler did it with the Jews we can run the risk of branding Muslims as subversives and terrorists, too. To be on the receiving end of this is painful and unfair. They whole point is to blame and then drive out, trying to get rid of the problem. In today's society, many do this rather than search inside themselves to examine how they each contribute to the problem.

The Hebrews had actual goats, hence the origin of our term 'scapegoat'. In Leviticus 16, the ritual of the scapegoat is laid out. Two goats are taken, one is sacrificed and one has hands laid upon it. The sins of the people are symbolically transferred to it and it is sent out into the wilderness. The blood of the first animal is taken by the high priest into the Holy Place and sprinkled before the ark of the covenant.

This happened once a year on Yom Kippur, the Day of Atonement, when the high priest entered behind the innermost veil before the glory of God and offered atonement for the sins of the people. Holman Hunt's painting of the scapegoat out in the wilderness captures the sense of isolation, fear and raging guilt that has been placed upon its shoulders.

And what of Jesus? He went into heaven, before the throne of God once and for all to make atonement for the sins of the world, presenting his blood (see Hebrews 9:24–25) and he was crucified outside the camp: 'And so Jesus also suffered outside the city gate to make the people holy through his own blood. Let us, then, go to him outside the camp, bearing the disgrace he bore' (Hebrews 13:12–13).

The difference in the case of Jesus when compared to all other scapegoats is that Jesus did return. By his resurrection, he broke the cycle of sin and death and returned to pour out forgiveness and to be the mediator of a new covenant. Through his blood alone we have equal access to the Father:

> For there is one God and one mediator between God and men, the man Christ Jesus. (1 Timothy 2:5)

PRAYER
Father, I thank you that Jesus is my peace, that he is the perfect sin offering, and the one who has totally given himself to you. He suffered and bled for me out of love, a love that made him come down and take flesh. I thank you that through him I can be cleansed, forgiven and set free. Through him I can be restored to life and the forces of darkness cannot contain him. Amen.

MEMORY VERSE

> It is the blood that makes atonement for one's life. (Leviticus 17:11)

Jesus in Numbers

The book of Numbers is about lists of tribes and ritual requirements. There are few narrative sections within this book. Jesus can be seen as foreshadowed in

- The rod that budded
- Water from the rock
- The bronze serpent
- Balaam's oracle

The Rod that Budded

Priest and Victim

Jesus is both priest and victim in the New Testament. He is the offerer and the thing offered. He goes into the heavens as high priest and makes atonement by offering his blood – the offerer and the sacrifice. In the well-known carol, 'We Three Kings of Orient Are' we find this sentiment in the following verse:

> Glorious now behold Him arise,
> King and God, and sacrifice!
> Heaven sings out 'Alleluia',
> 'Amen' the earth replies.
>
> (Revd John Henry Hopkins, dates unknown)

Aaron as high priest was a type of Jesus, the one who offers. The roles of prophet, priest and king are central to the Old Testament. The messianic oracles deal with the kingship of Jesus but there are important things to be said of the priestly and prophetic traditions, too. (More on the prophet in our study of Deuteronomy.) The story in Numbers 17 is first and foremost about the call of God upon Aaron and his vindication in the face of a rebellion against his authority, and that of Moses, by the sons of Korah. Each of the twelve tribes is told to place a staff before the Lord in the Holy Place. Aaron's is there for the tribe of Levi. The one that buds in the morning will be the rightful leader. Aaron's buds with blessing.

The blessing of God was upon Aaron's line, upon the priestly role in the old covenant until the Messiah came. So central was this that some of the Jews in the centuries before Jesus speculated that there would be two Messiahs, a priestly one and a kingly one! Jesus is the root and off-spring of David (see Revelation 22:16) but he is also the root and offspring of Aaron and the priestly line. Only in Jesus do we have total, bold access to the heavenly throne, offering his sacrifice that never needs to be reoffered.

Water from the Rock

The story of water flowing from the rock in Numbers 20 speaks of Jesus as living water (see John 4:13–14); Paul specifically equates the rock here with Jesus (see 1 Corinthians 10:3–4). So, Jesus is the rock and Jesus is the life-giving water. This is a double image, for from the rock of safety and faithful dependence, of divine security, flows salvation and redemption.

The Bronze Serpent

The story of the bronze serpent in Numbers 21 seems strange to our ears, perhaps. It seems that the Lord set up a talisman to avert sickness and death from the snakes that were troubling the Israelite camp. A bronze serpent was made and erected on a pole. Those who looked at this were healed. Moving on from the ritual exotica of the ancient days, we can see a moving image of the crucified Christ here. Jesus was set up on a tree, given for the life of the world. Jesus himself refers to this: 'But I, when I am lifted up from the earth, will draw all men unto myself' (John 12:32).

Lifting high the cross, preaching it, believing it, humbling ourselves before it, is powerful indeed. It is one of the secrets of a victorious Christian life and of effective evangelism. Lifting high the name of Jesus, too, is the secret of holy worship that helps to release the Holy Spirit in blessing. In one parish where I have served, there was unbelief, rebellion, people wanting a very 'C of E' cosy social club. My wife, after prayer about this frustrating situation, said, 'Just lift up the name of Jesus. Preach the gospel. Preach the cross. And sing his praises.' We adopted the chorus 'We Want to See Jesus Lifted High'. When we gathered and sang that and other holy songs, just a few in number, it was as though the heavens opened and things began to shift. Worship can be warfare.

Recently on English TV there has been a curious series called *Priest Idol*. This follows on, in name, from the popular series *Pop Idol* where unknown members of the public try out their talent and are trained up for a final contest. In *Priest Idol*, an American, Episcopalian priest took on a run-down northern English parish and a PR company was hired to give the place a facelift and to boost numbers. There were clever ideas and some obvious changes to be made to make new people feel welcome. There are common sense things that need to be done to foster renewal. However, that is where it stopped; slick gimmicks and bright ideas and a personable priest. That might work for a while or up to a point, but it is not the gospel. It won't change hearts or convict of a need for a saviour. Lifting high the cross and the name of Jesus will open the heavens and start things moving – no one can achieve this in their own strength.

Balaam's Oracle

The story of Balaam can be found in Numbers 22–24. Balak, son of the king of Moab, hired this seer to pronounce a curse upon Israel. Whenever he tried to mouth a curse, he could only utter a blessing, much to the chagrin of his employer. This story was a help and an encouragement to me some years ago in the parish I mentioned earlier. Part of this story was in the daily readings cycle that I was using at the time. The absolute inability to curse Israel leaped out at me and God spoke to me through this. I was going through difficult times and there was a group of influential parishioners who were determined to oust me – I was too much of a change and a threat. There was a horrible vendetta being waged and much character defamation. It was dark and evil. Balaam's experiences reassured me. If I was called by God to be in that place, if the anointing was upon me, then any curses would fail. And they did, praise be to God!

At the end of Balaam's oracles of blessing, he moves

prophetically, expressing an early form of the Messianic hope in vague and undefined terms:

> I see him, but not now;
>> I behold him, but not near.
> A star will come out of Jacob;
>> A sceptre will rise out of Israel. (Numbers 24:17)

One is to come, a ruler from Israel. The image of the star, a sign of power and divine appointment in those days, is also seen as echoing the Star of Bethlehem that guided the magi to the infant Jesus.

This oracle also shows how God can move sovereignly upon people outside of the church, or Israel. God is Lord of all the earth, and he will speak and raise up a witness where he will. Thus we have, today, stories of meditating Buddhists or gurus engaged in yoga who have a vision of the risen Jesus – or Muslims who live beyond the bounds of any possible missionary activity, and Jesus reveals himself to them in dreams and visions as *Isa al Masih*, his name in the Qur'an, and tells them to follow him; miraculous, sovereign and divine encounters that no one can engineer.

PRAYER

Father, I thank you that I have a faithful high priest who loves me eternally. Thank you that he has offered himself once for all to bring me into your presence. I thank you for that atoning sacrifice, that gift of love, that allows the water of life to bubble up within me, and allows Jesus to take his place at your right hand to reign for ever more, the expected, desired King of kings and Lord of lords. Amen.

MEMORY VERSE

A star will come out of Jacob;
A sceptre will rise out of Israel. (Numbers 24:17)

Jesus in Deuteronomy

Deuteronomy is a series of farewell speeches, teachings and blessings from Moses, rehearsing the key points of the Law. It is about the way of life and of death, of blessing and cursing. Various types of Jesus can be found within this book:

- Moses the deliverer
- The cities of refuge
- The prophet to come
- The tree and the curse

Moses the Deliverer

The role and figure of Moses himself is a type of Jesus. Moses was called to set the people free from slavery. He obeys and leads them out of Egypt and towards the borders of the Promised Land. Jesus is our deliverer, leading us out of bondage to sin and death. No other prophet in the Old Testament had such a key and foundational role as Moses, and yet Jesus goes further and does what he could not do. Moses was forbidden to enter the Promised Land because of his disobedience when water came from the rock. He had been told to speak to the rock and yet he hit it with his staff (Numbers 20:6–13). On the surface, he does not enter the promise because of sin, but a deeper

reading would suggest that the Law (which Moses repre-
sented) could lead into the promise of the gospel. It is a
schoolmaster pointing the way, but it has no power to
change hearts and to save. So much came through Moses,
but so much more came through Jesus.

> For the law was given through Moses; grace and truth
> came through Jesus Christ.   (John 1:17)

> Moses was faithful as a servant in all God's house, testify-
> ing to what would be said in the future. But Christ is
> faithful as a son over God's house.   (Hebrews 3:5–6a)

This weight of glory, of redemption, in Jesus is captured
poetically in these words of Ambrose of Milan, a fifth-cen-
tury bishop. He imagines Mary, hesitating, trembling, before
the angel Gabriel at the annunciation (see Luke 1:26–38):

> And behold, to you the price of our salvation is offered. If
> you consent, straightaway, shall we be freed. Adam asks
> this of you, O loving Virgin... Abraham begs this of you,
> and David, this all the holy fathers implore... And rightly
> so, for on your lips is hanging the consolation of the
> wretched, the redemption of the captive, the speedy deliv-
> erance of all who otherwise are lost, in a word, the salva-
> tion of all Adam's children, of all your race.
>
> Answer, O Virgin, answer the angel speedily... Speak
> the word and receive the Word; offer what is yours and
> conceive what is of God... Why delay? Why tremble?
> Believe, speak, receive! Let your humility put on boldness
> and your modesty be clothed with trust. Open your lips to
> speak, open your bosom to your Maker. Behold, the
> Desired of all nations is outside, knocking at your door.
> Arise then, run and open. Open by your word. And Mary

said, 'Behold the handmaid of the Lord: be it done to me according to your word.'[1]

This moving meditation on the annunciation story captures the sense of the longing of the people of Israel, of the old covenant saints. They longed for Messiah's day, for the 'Desired of all nations'. In some traditions, it is believed that they had to wait in Sheol, the Underworld, until Jesus died and rose again. Then he set them free and led them into the joys of heaven. The Eastern churches paint a vivid and colourful icon of this event, with Jesus rising up, clutching Adam's wrist and leading others with him in triumphal procession. Others question this interpretation, pointing to Scriptures that indicate that the Old Testament saints were in the presence of God after their deaths, such as Jesus' teaching about the Lord calling himself 'the God of Abraham... Isaac and... Jacob' (see Mark 12:18–27).

Whatever the truth of the above, Jesus is the fulfilment. He is a son over the house rather than a servant, to quote Hebrews. In Roman law the son inherited; a servant did not. Jesus has greater power and glory. Another way of expressing this in Hebrews 4 is that the promised rest of the people of God comes about only in Jesus – the Hebrews moaned and wandered in the wilderness; Moses failed to enter the Promised Land; troubles beset the tribes once settled. The rest of God is a rest from all strife and guilt, a rest from trying to earn God's favour, safe in the loving arms of the Father, accepted, forgiven, loved.

There remains, then, a Sabbath-rest for the people of God; for anyone who enters God's rest also rests from his own work, just as God did from his.   (Hebrews 4:9)

The Divine Office: Vol. 1, London: Collins, 1974

Moses could not lead the people into this; Jesus can.

The Cities of Refuge

In Deuteronomy 4:41–43, three cities of refuge are designated, Bezer, Gilead and Golan. The idea was that if a man killed his neighbour accidentally, without malicious forethought, then he could flee to these places to escape tribal vendettas of 'an eye for an eye' while the priests looked into his case. After a period of time, he could then return home if he was declared innocent. These were practical and caring arrangements in such a tribal society, but some see a type of Christ in these. Jesus is our place of safety that we must flee to for mercy, protection and forgiveness. We can come to Jesus, though, even when we are guilty, even when we have sinned wilfully. This message of grace is staggering for some when it is first heard. Think of the story of conversions of notorious sinners such as Nicky Cruz. He hated himself and God, and the preacher David Wilkerson. He had killed and robbed, hurt and done drugs and slept around. The unconditional love that Wilkerson showed him, representing Jesus, eventually melted his heart and the Holy Spirit did his work. Or think of the former slave trader in the eighteenth century, John Newton. He could not believe that a hard-hearted man such as he could be forgiven, and the hymn 'Amazing Grace' was penned in thankful praise:

Amazing grace (how sweet the sound)
that saved a wretch like me!
I once was lost, but now am found,
was blind, but now I see.   (John Newton, 1725–1807)

The Prophet to Come

Moses promised that God would send a prophet like him to lead the people:

> The Lord your God will raise up for you a prophet like me from among your own brothers. You must listen to him.
> (Deuteronomy 18:15)

In context, this was a warning to trust the Lord and not to seek after fortune-tellers and spiritualists. Moses meant that others prophets would come. But the singular form aroused speculations. Was this a special, messianic figure? Would there be a prophet Messiah as well as a king Messiah? For Christians, Jesus is the fulfilment of this par excellence. He is the one of whom God has spoken in all his fullness. He is the Word made flesh. Others heard the word; he was and is the Word.

The Tree and the Curse

Deuteronomy 21:23 says, 'anyone who is hung on a tree is under God's curse'. This referred to the practice of exposing bodies of executed criminals on a tree in public, overnight, to shame them and their families. The Law says to take them down before nightfall or there will be a curse. This law might have been humanitarian, to prevent such disgraceful exposure. Later Jewish writers debated whom the curse rested upon – was it the deceased or those who put the body on the tree? Some said the former (e.g. the Qumran community), and some the latter (i.e. the rabbis). Paul is original in seeing a type of Christ here, linking this with the cross and the death of the Messiah. Jesus became a curse for us:

> Christ redeemed us from the curse of the law by becoming a curse for us. (Galatians 3:13)

The idea of Jesus becoming a curse, by taking sin upon himself on the cross, is striking. Again, we see the horror of evil, the wickedness of our rebellion that Jesus stares in the face and absorbs, cancelling it and redeeming us. It is another way of saying that God in Christ took our punishment upon himself. This reminds me of a Christian who visited Auschwitz and hesitated before walking into the crematoria. She heard the whisper of God's voice reassuring her: 'There is nowhere that I cannot go, and nowhere that I have not been.' In Jesus, we see this most clearly.

PRAYER

Father, I thank you that what the Law could not do, grace can do. I thank you that I can enter the promises of God through Jesus, covered with his blood. I thank you that I can come to him unworthy and lost, to be found, loved and healed. I thank you for his guidance, for hearing your Word and his voice, and I thank you that he took my punishment, becoming a curse for me, and loved me despite my sin. Amen.

MEMORY VERSE

> The Lord your God will raise up for you a prophet like me from among your brothers. You must listen to him. (Deuteronomy 18:15)

PART TWO –

Jesus in the Historical Books

The Historical books of the Old Testament are so classified because they cover the stories of the conquest of Canaan and the reigns of various kings. The idea of the coming Messiah becomes firmer as the people have anointed kings ruling over them. There are also mighty men and prophets who are moved by the Spirit of God, the Temple in Jerusalem, as well as various images of redemption and deliverance. All of these speak of Jesus as the coming King, empowered by the Spirit, the dwelling place of God and the great Redeemer.

Jesus in Joshua

Joshua deals with the initial entry into Canaan by the Israelite tribes. They are led by Moses' successor, Joshua. Items which are types of Jesus are:

- The name 'Joshua'
- The land as the place of promise and rest
- Death and resurrection seen in the crossing of the Jordan
- The Captain of the Lord of Hosts
- The scarlet cord

The name 'Joshua'

The first type of Christ is the name of the leader, Joshua. This means 'Yah Saves' or 'The Lord Saves'. It is the Hebrew form of 'Jesus', in fact. Here a man is sent, empowered by the Spirit, to take enemy territory. Jesus was sent from the Father to save humanity from sin, death and the devil. C.S. Lewis comments in his books that this was an invasion as Jesus entered into enemy occupied territory. He was writing in the Second World War years, of course, and this image was even more poignant. I have often thought that a novel way to make a new Jesus movie would be to follow the format of a heist story like *Ocean's*

Eleven. Jesus came to gather a team of helpers and to take the kingdom from Satan.

Recently, I listened to a preacher comparing Islam with Christianity. He commented on the ninety-nine beautiful names of Allah, which are found in the Qur'an, such as 'Compassionate' or 'Light'. These are actually very sound and wonderful, but there is at least one lacking, that of 'Saviour'. Nowhere in the Qur'an is Allah ever described as saving his people. In fact, there is no saviour figure in any of the world's religions – there might be teachers, prophets, revealers, but never a saviour. Christianity is unique in this respect as God steps into his creation to rescue us by sheer grace.

This type found in the name of Joshua should alert us that in this book there will be various symbols and suggestions about the coming of Jesus and the spiritual battle involved.

The Land as the Place of Promise and Rest

The Israelites needed a land to settle in after living a nomadic existence in the Negev. Their ancestors had come from Canaan, but now the situation was rather different. Powerful city-states ruled the land, headed by kings. They exacted taxes in a feudal system that kept many of the old Semitic stock in servitude. There were going to be head-on conflicts if the Israelites wanted territory, and scholars speculate that some of the common people welcomed them as kinsmen and liberators. The land serves as a metaphor, also, for the place of promise and rest. Canaan is spoken of as 'the Promised Land' where the tribes come to an end of their wanderings. Hebrews picks up on this with the idea of entering God's rest:

Therefore, since the promise of entering his rest still stands, let us be careful that none of you be found to have fallen short of it. For if Joshua had given them rest, God would not have spoken later about another day. There remains, then, a Sabbath-rest for the people of God; for anyone who enters God's rest also rests from his own work, just as God did from his.   (Hebrews 4:1, 8–10)

The author of Hebrews plays with the image of the Sabbath day rest when God finished creation, and the entering into the Promised Land. Both are images of coming rest. In Jesus, the believer finds rest from striving to please God. There is a place of peace and of promise:

Therefore, since we have been justified through faith, we have peace with God through our Lord Jesus Christ.
(Romans 5:1)

For no matter how many promises God has made, they are all 'Yes' in Christ.   (2 Corinthians 1:20)

Crossing the Jordan

The generation who had passed through the Red Sea had all died; the next generation needed their own 'baptism' as they crossed through the waters of the Jordan with a similar miracle. The priests led the way with ark of the covenant, a symbol of Jesus, bearing the Shekinah, the presence or glory of God. Going down into the river and coming up again suggested a dying and a rising. In the Old Testament there was a close link between these two waters. For example, the Psalms linked them thus:

> Why was it, O sea, that you fled,
> O Jordan, that you turned back. (Psalm 114:5)

This also suggests that 'God has no grandchildren' as the old saying goes. He has sons only, people who have come to know him for themselves. This might happen in numerous ways – no two testimonies are exactly the same. Believing parents and relatives might bring them before the Lord, bring them into worship, and educate them, but at the end of the day, somehow, sometime, the children need to own the faith for themselves and have their own encounter with the risen Lord.

That entrance is a dying and a rising:

> I have been crucified with Christ and I no longer live, but Christ lives in me. The life I live in the body, I live by faith in the Son of God, who loved me and gave himself for me.
> (Galatians 2:20)

The Captain of the Lord of Hosts

Joshua speaks often of conflict, struggle and spiritual warfare. The land is enemy occupied territory and so is the whole earth. It is under the dominion of Satan according to the New Testament:

> Again the devil took him to a very high mountain and showed him all the kingdoms of the world and their splendour. 'All this I will give you,' he said, 'if you will bow down and worship me.' (Matthew 4:8–9)

Joshua 5:13–15 is set just before the conquest of Jericho. Joshua has a vision of an angelic being who reassures him that the Lord will be with the Israelites. It is a shattering vision of holiness. Who is this captain? Some suggest that it is the archangel Michael who fights Satan in Revelation or who struggled with the demonic prince of Persia in the book of Daniel. Maybe. This figure is akin to the enigmatic 'Angel of the Lord' in the Torah. He commands Joshua to take off his shoes for it is holy ground, a command similar to that given to Moses by the Lord at the burning bush. Elsewhere angels object when people bow or fall on the ground before them as they are not objects of worship (see Revelation 19:9–10).

Perhaps this captain is a form of the pre-existent Christ, the Son or the Word in visionary form. In these early parts of the Old Testament, angels are little spoken of apart from this strong figure that seems to be an extension of God, a manifestation of God to the people. The captain holds a strong sword as a symbol of strength and judgement; Jesus when he returns has a sword that comes from his mouth in Revelation 19:15.

The Scarlet Cord

Joshua 2:17–21 relates the story of Rahab's oath to hang a scarlet cord from her window as a sign that she was under the protection of the Israelite tribes. She had sheltered the Israelite spies and allowed them to escape. When Jericho fell, she and her family were spared (see Joshua 6:22–23). This scarlet cord was recognized as a type of the blood of Jesus as long ago as the late first century AD in the writings of Clement of Rome. This early bishop of Rome wrote a section about Rahab in his first epistle to the Corinthians. He praises Rahab for the virtue of hospitality, welcoming the people of God and his word. Then he comments upon the cord:

> They went on to give her a sign, telling her she was to hang out a scarlet cord from her house – thereby typifying the redemption which all who put their trust and hope in God shall find, through the blood of the Lord. (Notice, dear friends. How in this woman there was not only faith, but prophecy also.)
>
> (*The First Epistle of Clement to the Corinthians 12*)[1]

Rahab is praised for her hospitality and in this we see an open heart, a willing spirit, obedience and submission to the word of God. She is the good and fertile soil in the parable of the sower who responds. So much has been given, so much mercy poured out by grace, but not all can open up and receive it. It has been said that God pours out his love and salvation over the world, but it is like a jug of water being poured into smaller pots. Those with the lids on cannot receive it.

This scarlet cord is used as the leitmotif of the Old Testament by Richard Booker in his *The Miracle of the Scarlet Thread*.[2] The theme of blood redemption, of the love that makes atonement for us, made the Hebrew Bible come alive for him. It is the thread woven throughout all the pages of the Bible:

> ... from Genesis to Revelation, the Bible tells one story. The story is that God has entered into a BLOOD

---

1 *The First Epistle of Clement to the Corinthians 12*, translated by J.B. Lightfoot, adapted and modernised © 1990 Athena Data Products.

2 Richard Booker, *The Miracle of the Scarlet Thread*, PA: Destiny Image Publishers Inc., 1988.

COVENANT with man through the Lord Jesus Christ. And all who will, may enter into the covenant with Him.

Here we see the theme of hospitality again. Open hearts to receive the gift of God.

Clement also says that prophecy as well as faith was in Rahab, and it is so in many Old Testament characters. Their stories speak of Jesus, but the modern reader may well ask if such small details as a scarlet cord were actually, deliberately, prophetic details. Was it a happy coincidence, being read into the story by later believers, or was it intended as a prophetic symbol? Perhaps we cannot answer that, but it is there, and we can see a sign of the blood covenant there. It would be an amazing coincidence, wouldn't it?

PRAYER

Father, I praise you that one of your names is 'Saviour', that you have not left us helpless, but have come to us in your mercy. I thank you that by grace we can pass through cleansing and death to our flesh, embracing the cross and rising in the resurrection. I thank you that we can find peace in you and inherit all the promises of the Bible in Jesus. I can enter into rest from all my striving, accepted in the beloved. I can come under the protection of Jesus as my captain and take the land. I thank you for the wonder of redemption, for the blood shed for me and for the salvation offered to the world. Amen.

MEMORY VERSE

The men said to her, 'This oath you made us swear will not be binding on us unless, when we enter the land, you have tied this scarlet cord in the window through which you let us down, and unless you have brought your father, and mother, your brothers and all your family into your house...' (Joshua 2:17–18)

Jesus in Judges

Judges tells of the early settlement in Canaan by the Israelite tribes and their trials and tribulations. The tribes form a confederation without a regular leader. Leaders, 'judges', are raised up by the call of God.

Four things speak of Jesus in this book:

- The judges as deliverers
- Choosing the weak to bring salvation
- The Angel of the Lord
- The jars and torches

The Judges as Deliverers

Remembering the words of Richard Booker, there is one story told in the Bible, that of redemption. A verse from Isaiah shows this:

> When they cry out to the Lord because of their oppressors, he will send them a saviour and defender, and he will rescue them. (Isaiah 19:20b)

There were twelve judges, though we are told next to nothing about some of them, such as Tola who had control for twenty-three years! One was a woman, Deborah. They were called and empowered in times of crisis, when the tribes had forsaken the Lord and were doing as each one saw fit. They were attacked and at the mercy of the Philistines, the Moabites or the Midianites who were the neighbouring powers, as well as Canaanite city-state coalitions. The Lord was true to his covenant and he came to the aid of his people when they turned to him. This is an extension of the name 'Saviour' that Joshua bore. His successors carried on the salvation of God.

Choosing the Weak to Bring Salvation

Some of the judges showed flaws and either moral or physical weakness. Ehud (Judges 3:12–30) was left-handed, a social stigma of the day. Deborah (Judges 4–5) was a woman, and women were not expected to hold authority or take charge of military strategy. Gideon (Judges 6:1–8:35) felt unworthy as he was from a poor family and was the poorest member of that family: ' "But Lord," Gideon asked, "how can I save Israel? My clan is the weakest in Manasseh, and I am the least in my family." The Lord answered, "I will be with you, and you will strike down all the Midianites together" ' (Judges 6:15–16). Samson (Judges 13:1–16:31) was morally weak, falling for the wiles of Delilah so that the Spirit left him and he failed. He was given a second chance at the end of his life.

In these stories we see the weakness of the incarnation. 'The Word became flesh' (John 1:14) and humbled himself to take the form of a servant (Philippians 2:6–8). God often chooses the weak people to stop any human pride. I am only too glad of this grace for my calling as a priest and pastor does not rest upon my natural skills. I might be able to listen and teach, but I know the grace that has cleansed me, empowered me and called me. Without this

I could not have taken the steps in life that I have done. Thank God for the cross and the power of the Holy Spirit! I knew what it was to lack confidence with people as a young man and love has shaped me and changed me along the way. When we are empty, how much more he can fill us.

The Angel of the Lord

The Angel of the Lord appeared to Gideon on the threshing floor: 'The Lord is with you, mighty warrior' (Judges 6:12), he says, and as the narrative proceeds, the angel and the Lord seem to be synonymous. Thus we hear, 'The Lord turned to him and said...' (Judges 6:14). Again, we see a close link between the figure of the angel and the pre-existent Christ. Commentators differ over this. Are we dealing with an angelic being, a theophany (a symbolic appearance of God), or the pre-existent Christ?

The Jars and Torches

As well as the other three things in this book that speak of Jesus, we may see him in the jars and torches. Judges 7 tells the story of how Gideon defeated the Midianites. He had his men hide burning torches inside clay jars. They waited until nightfall and then blew trumpets to waken and startle the enemy. Then the men broke the jars and brandished the torches. Disorientated, the Midianites believed that many more men than there were surrounded them. Some see the torches hidden in the clay jars as prefiguring the incarnation. Jesus was God in the flesh, or as Wesley put it, 'veiled in flesh the Godhead see!... incarnate Deity' (Charles Wesley, 1707–88). God entered his creation in a hidden manner, confounding the enemy of our souls, Satan, and invading his territory.

PRAYER

Father, I thank you that you are our strong deliverer, that when we call out to you, you answer. Thank you that you choose the weak things of this world to shame the rich. In my weakness I can know your strength. It is not I, but Christ who lives in me. I can do all things through Christ who strengthens me. Thank you that you go before me and lead me in the path that I should go. I praise you for Jesus coming in the flesh to be my redeemer. Amen.

MEMORY VERSE

The Lord is with you, mighty warrior.   (Judges 6:12)

Jesus in Ruth

Ruth is a short book of the Old Testament set in the days of the judges. It is about the fortunes and loyalty of a foreign woman who embraces the God of Israel. There are themes of blessing, rescue and raising the royal seed. Jesus is prefigured in

- The kinsman-redeemer
- The royal seed
- Bethlehem

The Kinsman-Redeemer

The *go'el*, or 'kinsman-redeemer', is a key figure in Ruth. She returns with Naomi, her mother-in-law, to eke out a paltry existence gathering stalks of corn that were left in the fields by the workmen. She attracts the attention of the owner of the field, Boaz, a kinsman of her deceased husband. She seeks him out as he sleeps on the threshing floor after the harvest. He spreads his blanket over her to keep her warm and protect her, a symbol of his claim and his protection. We are covered, in turn, with the protection of the blood of Jesus as his claim is laid upon us: 'But now in Christ Jesus you who were once far away have been brought near through the blood of Christ. For he himself is our peace' (Ephesians 2:13–14a); 'Be shepherds of the church of God, which he bought with his own blood' (Acts 20:28).

There is another kinsman who is closer in line to claim her. Boaz and he barter and he gives way to Boaz, who takes her as his wife.

The tradition of the *go'el* is based upon the idea of brothers taking their kinsmen's widows and taking them into their home and siring children through them (see Deuteronomy 25:5–10).

The Royal Seed

Ruth gave birth to Obed, who became the grandfather of King David. David was of the royal, messianic line. Ruth's redemption by Boaz thus contributed to God's grand plan that unravels gradually in the Old Testament. Jesus as 'Son of David' is acknowledged as the Messiah in the New Testament. Thus Paul could declare: 'regarding his Son, who as to his human nature was a descendant of David' (Romans 1:3).

It is amazing that the messianic line came through a Gentile woman, a Moabitess. This shows the grace and mercy of God, gathering the nations to him, and this pre-figures the universal salvation brought by Jesus. The new covenant extends beyond the people of Israel.

Bethlehem

Ruth returned to Bethlehem, for that was where her husband's family came from. There she married Boaz and gave birth to one of the royal line of the Messiah. Bethlehem, the 'house of bread', was a fitting symbol for the birthplace of the Messiah, for Bethlehem was to be the birthplace of Jesus, too, prophesied as such in the Prophets. There is no prediction in Ruth, just the mention of the place. This is where the action and the blessing takes place – a small place that was rather insignificant in those days. Such is God's way, moving by grace in great humility, choosing the small places and people to bring great blessing. He is no respecter of geography and merely seeks hearts that are open to him, but many great revivals have happened in out-of-the-way places, small towns or amongst the most unlikely people. A New Zealand preacher friend of mine was present at such an outpouring in a tiny farming community in the USA. There were just about 300 people and the place was a simple crossroads. There in a small Methodist church, great blessings and healings broke out and the people began to travel to see what was happening. Why not in New York? We do not know, but faithful people had prayed for many years and in that tiny, way-out place, God moved. The great Pentecostal revival began in a garage in Los Angeles in 1906 through the prayers and witness of a one-eyed black man, William Seymour. God moves in the humble, little people and places:

> Now to him who is able to do immeasurably more than we can ask or imagine, according to his power that is at work within us, to him be glory in the church and in Christ Jesus throughout all generations, for ever and ever! Amen. (Ephesians 3:20–21)

PRAYER

Father, I thank you that you are my redeemer. You rescued me when I needed help; you spread your garment over me and cover me with the precious blood of Jesus. I thank you that we are adopted into the royal family of Jesus and know all his saving benefits. Thank you that you move when we are empty and humble, surrendering all to you. Amen.

MEMORY VERSE

'I am your servant Ruth', she said. 'Spread the corner of your garment over me, since you are a kinsman-redeemer.'   (Ruth 3:9)

Jesus in 1 and 2 Samuel

The books of Samuel describe the end of the period of the judges and the beginning of the monarchy. With the establishment of the monarchy, the role and figure of the Messiah becomes more focused. Jesus is prefigured in these books as:

- God's Son
- The anointed king
- The intercessor
- Jonathan risking his life
- David, the shepherd and king
- The promised son

God's Son

The story of Hannah's gift of her son, Samuel, to the Lord in 1 Samuel 1–2 is one that tugs at the heartstrings. You can't help reading through this without feeling the pain of a thousand mothers – mothers who have undergone an abortion and live with the regret and guilt afterwards; mothers who have lost a child through cot death or illness or road accidents; mothers who have miscarried or women who are infertile. And you can't help reading through this section of Scripture without feeling that God knows the pain that mothers can go through. This was impressed upon me so deeply one year when preparing this reading for a Mothering Sunday service. I felt the heavy compassion of God for these women. I sensed the same when on a retreat in Ireland with members of Rachel's Vineyard. This group works with women who have had abortions and cannot forgive themselves. Maybe they have kept it secret. It weights heavily and causes many problems. Often they have been told, as young women, that this will not harm them and that the embryos are not real people yet. Still, their grief is real and after many years in some cases, it seeps out to the surface. A caring Irish Catholic priest, Father Pat Scanlon, introduced me to this group and I investigated it further at his invitation. He said to me, 'Ah, you can't go far wrong, now, if you preach mercy!' These are women who cry for their children like Rachel, mentioned in Jeremiah 31:15. The retreats are beautiful affairs with Gospel meditations, sharing times, little rituals and symbols of hope, and a time when lost babies can be named and a final memorial service is held for them. There the tears flow and deep release is found. The beauty of the Gospel is not only that the mothers can know forgiveness, but that they have the hope of seeing their children one day in heaven, the 'Holy Innocents' as they are known in the Catholic tradition. I was privileged to attend one such retreat with an agnostic woman of great depth and intelligence who was moved, found some healing and was left wondering about Jesus and the whole 'Church' thing. The symbol for Rachel's Vineyard is a teardrop shaped pearl with angels' wings. The tears of the mothers (and fathers) find hope in the kingdom of heaven. Strong principles and teachings do not rule out mercy for those that fail, just as in the story of the woman brought before Jesus who was an adulterer.

'Does no one condemn you?' he asked. 'Then neither do I. Go, and sin no more.'

Hannah makes a vow to surrender her son to the Lord if she gets pregnant. Yes, she has more children and is fruitful and blessed, but her firstborn is given up. He is brought up in the Temple and trained by the priest Eli. The name 'Samuel' is often translated 'Hear God' as Samuel as a boy heard the voice of the Lord calling him. The Hebrew form probably derives from the Assyrian word *summu* meaning 'son'. Hence, Hannah named her boy 'Son of God' as she was handing him over totally into his care. In the story of Hannah and Samuel, there is a type of Mary and Jesus. Hannah is infertile and conceives naturally after prayer; Mary receives a miracle in her womb while still a virgin. Hannah sings a song of thanksgiving to the Lord, as does Mary in the Magnificat. Jesus was 'Son of God' in a fuller, richer sense.

The Anointed King

In Hannah's song she exclaims, 'He will give strength to his king and exalt the horn of his anointed' (1 Samuel 2:10b).

1 Samuel is concerned with describing the origin of the monarchy in Israel. The people demand a king from Samuel as other nations around them have such a ruler. The Israelite confederacy of tribes depended upon cooperation and the chrism of a spiritually anointed leader or judge. The judges were not dynastic. The tribes saw hope in establishing a dynasty for then everyone knew where they were and who was in charge. Samuel felt that this was rejecting the Lord as King and he warned the people what this would mean. Still, they were granted their wish. Saul was chosen prophetically and anointed with holy oil.

All of this goes disastrously wrong as Saul does not listen and rebels until he loses his life in battle. In 2 Samuel 2, David is anointed king over the people. Earlier, when Samuel realized that the Lord had rejected Saul, he anointed David as the future king, in private. He looked at the sons of Jesse and prayed for a word from the Lord to reveal the new king. Something was wrong; one was missing. The family dismissed him, as he was the youngest. Yet, David was chosen, again showing that God often chooses the weak things of this world, and looks on the heart and not on outward appearance.

Jesus stood in the royal line. He was anointed, not with a horn of holy oil, but by the oil of the Holy Spirit. At the baptism of Jesus, when the Spirit descended upon him, he heard the Father's voice saying: 'You are my Son, whom I love; with you I am well pleased' (Mark 1:11).

The Intercessor

Samuel as high priest stood before the Lord and prayed for his people. He was an intercessor whose prayers were powerful. Later in the Old Testament, the power of such prayers is acknowledged: 'Even if Moses and Samuel were to stand before me, my heart would not go out to this people' (Jeremiah 15:1).

Jesus is revealed as our high priest in Hebrews, interceding for us. (See Hebrews 4:14–16; also, Romans 8:34.)

Jonathan risking his Life

Jonathan, Saul's son, befriended the rebel David and secretly helped him. They made a covenant together to support each other and Jonathan stripped off his royal robes and his sword. These he gave to David as a sign of protection and honour. Jonathan often risked his life to aid David, sneaking behind his father's back. Three times we are told of the covenant that the two made – 1 Samuel 18:3; 20:15–16 and 23:18. In this we see the faithfulness and vulnerability of Jesus. God became incarnate in the child in the manger, putting himself into the care of Mary's hands, being born in the squalor of the stable. He laid aside his majesty to save us. This is captured in the early Christian hymn which Paul quotes in Philippians 2:5–11: '… but made himself nothing, taking the very nature of a servant…'

How much we are worth, to have Jesus give his life for us! There is a story told of the late Dr Francis Schaeffer, a Swiss pastor and philosopher, who was walking through Paris with some of his students. They were shocked to see him walk up to a prostitute on a street corner. He asked her what she charged.

More shock! She wanted $50. 'Too cheap!' he countered. She kept upping the price and he kept saying it was too little until she blurted out, 'How much do you think I am worth to you, then?' He replied that he couldn't possibly pay her what she was really worth, but he could introduce her to someone who could. There and then, he spoke about Jesus and they both ended up kneeling on the pavement to pray.

David, the Shepherd and King

David was chosen from among his brothers as the future king. He was a shepherd boy, and the image emerges in the Old Testament of the Messiah as shepherd and king: 'I will place over them one shepherd, my servant David' (Ezekiel 34:23).

We also see David's magnetism for the malcontents, for the waifs and strays: 'All those who were in distress or in debt or discontented gathered round him, and he became their leader' (1 Samuel 22:2a). Jesus gathered the outcasts of his day, the prostitutes, tax collectors and lepers, showing them compassion. Jesus called himself the good shepherd: 'I am the good shepherd. The good shepherd lays down his life for the sheep' (John 10:11).

There is a sign of spiritual life in a church that is unmissable. It is not just about the worship or the preaching or the crowds, but the type of people who are being attracted. I remember a wildcat preacher years ago who said that when he met the Holy Spirit his life and ministry changed. His local church knew when some of his friends entered. They were the difficult ones, the tramps, the hookers, the addicts, the homeless, the broken and the crying. The love of God bade him welcome them and they were drawn to the presence of mercy like a magnet.

The Promised Son

The prophet Nathan had a word from God for David in 2 Samuel 7. David was not going to be the one who built a Temple for the Lord. Up until that time the ark had rested in the tabernacle tent, moving from place to place. Now it was in Jerusalem, David's capital and the place of his throne. Still, Nathan said, the Lord would raise up his offspring to build a House for the Lord:

> ...I will raise up your offspring to succeed you, who will come from your own body, and I will establish his

kingdom. He is the one who will build a house for my Name, and I will establish the throne of his kingdom for ever. I will be his father, and he shall be my son.

(2 Samuel 7:12–14a)

In one sense, David's actual son, Solomon, fulfilled this prophecy. He was the most successful Israelite king and he built the first Temple. However, his line came to an end with the rise of Rome and the kingship has never been restored to Israel. However, Jesus as Messiah, the anointed high priest and King, fulfils these hopes. His throne will never end and the house for the name that he has built will last for ever. This house is his own body, the risen body of the Lord: 'Jesus answered them, "Destroy this temple and I will raise it again in three days."… But the temple he had spoken of was his body' (John 2:19–21).

PRAYER

Father, I praise you that you know the pain of mothers who have lost their children. You bind up the broken-hearted and bring the balm of forgiveness. You, too, know the pain of loss, and endured separation from your Son on the cross. Thank you that Jesus, the precious and risen Son, intercedes for us, and that he stripped himself of his glory to save us and win our hearts. Thank you that he has made a covenant written in blood never to forsake us. Thank you that he is my shepherd and our King, and I bow before his majesty and embrace the glory of his everlasting throne. Amen.

MEMORY VERSE

I will establish the throne of his kingdom for ever. I will be his father, and he shall be my son.

(2 Samuel 7:24)

Jesus in 1 and 2 Kings

The books of Kings describe the progress of the monarchy under Solomon and then the schism that occurred as the nation split into two kingdoms, those of Israel and Judah. The various fortunes of the different kings are followed. Some are faithful to the covenant with the Lord and some are not. First the Assyrians and then the Babylonians bring disaster. The northern tribes were swept away by the former power, and Judah by the latter. Only Judah was to return.

Various themes and stories speak of Jesus, besides the role of the anointed king:

- Solomon's wisdom
- Elisha the healer
- Naaman's cleansing
- The royal seed

Solomon's Wisdom

The wisdom of Solomon was, and is, legendary:

God gave Solomon wisdom and very great insight, and a breadth of understanding as measureless as the sand on the seashore. Solomon's wisdom was greater than the

wisdom of all the men of the East, and greater than all the
wisdom of Egypt.   (1 Kings 4:29–30)

His reign was an era of peace, 'the Lord my God has given
me rest on every side' (1 Kings 5:4).

Wisdom, as will be seen later, was a major theme in the
developing Old Testament Scriptures. Wisdom is a guide
for living, a respect for the Lord, and an approach to
health of mind, body and spirit. Jesus is described as the
wisdom of God incarnate, 'Christ the power of God and
the wisdom of God' (1 Corinthians 1:24).

Wisdom is, in fact, personified poetically in various Old
Testament verses.

In Jesus we see the guide to life, the way to the Father,
the path to peace and the healing presence of God: 'I am
the way and the truth and the life. No-one comes to the
Father except through me' (John 14:6). And to this wisdom, people are drawn like bees to a honeypot: 'Men of all
nations came to listen to Solomon's wisdom, sent by all
the kings of the world, who had heard his wisdom' (1
Kings 4:34). The most striking of these admirers and seekers was the Queen of Sheba.

People are drawn to the wise. When there is a dilemma,
a wise leader will be listened to and things will fall into
place. In Jesus, we sense the answer to life and we are
drawn. When people sense that he is honoured and that
his Spirit is at work, then they will want to come to a fellowship or a church and seek to belong. Then you don't
need to force, cajole or entertain them. Gimmicks are
redundant when Jesus is in the house. This makes me
think of the time when I started in my present parish.
There was a monthly family service that was well
attended, but it soon became obvious that I was expected

to be an entertainer. We tried to think of a better gimmick and trick month after month – cycling down the aisle as a French bread-seller, bringing a see-saw into church, spinning plates and dressing people up – and then I stopped it. It wasn't going anywhere. No real commitment, no devotion. There was no desire to belong. A bit of fun with a moral and then as the kids got older, they dropped out altogether.

Instead, a new service was started that gathered around modern worship, teaching from the Bible, and a simple communion. Alpha courses began and we prayed for change. Then the first real converts started coming. There is now a committed core of forty or so adults, and their children, who are switched on, hungry for biblical teaching, Holy Spirit ministry and also respectful of the sacraments. I had to let a pantomime go and slowly build something deeper. The new people want to be there, as often as they can. They belong, they are drawn to worship, they know the Lord and they want to be with each other. You will find them sharing and hugging, praying over coffee with people. How different that is.

Elisha the Healer

Many wonderful stories are told of Elisha's healings in 2 Kings. In chapter 4, for example, he prays for the woman of Shunem that she might have a son. She does, but later, he takes ill and dies. She calls for the man of God and he prays over the boy, lying on him and feeling warmth return to the boy. The delighted mother gave thanks to God.

Elisha had a double portion of his old master, Elijah's, anointing. Jesus was anointed more than any other, as the

Holy Spirit filled him to overflowing. In him all the fullness of God dwelled (Colossians 1:19). Healings abounded
in his presence. When John's disciples asked Jesus if he
really were the expected Messiah, he answered: 'Go back
and report to John what you hear and see: The blind
receive sight, the lame walk, those who have leprosy are
cured, the deaf hear, the dead are raised, and the good
news is preached to the poor' (Matthew 11:4–5).

As we live in a fallen world, 'between the ages', we do
not always see the answers to prayer that we would like.
Healing is a reality, but a mystery in the Body of Christ. I
have seen many different healing ministries with their different approaches and angles, but the one thing that
impresses more than results is compassion. There are
cures, experiences and amazing things. My own wife was
healed (very unemotionally as other people around her
were falling over, shaking or laughing) of fibromyalgia.
That was absolutely brilliant, but what do we do with the
people who receive prayer but are not healed? That is the
test of our Christianity. They need love and support, and
many can find great inner strength to cope through this
affirmation as well as through the laying on of hands.

Perhaps we have to deal with the agony of living in a
fallen world and the sovereignty of God. We don't have all
the answers, but we do know that God can heal, and that
this poured through Jesus, and is still at work.

Naaman's Cleansing

In 2 Kings 5, we read the story of the Aramean comman-
der, Naaman. He heard of the holy man, Elisha, and asked
him for help, as he had leprosy. Elisha could have just
prayed for him but he gave him some unusual

instructions. He had to go and wash seven times in the River Jordan. As if bathing in front of his men wasn't enough, it had to be a river in Judea and not Syria. Yet, after a fit of anger and frustration, Naaman obeyed and bathed. After seven dips, the leprosy cleared up.

This incident shows the need for humility and offering of self, and the cleansing power of the Holy Spirit. The cleansing work of the cross is prefigured, to a degree, in this incident. 'But if we walk in the light, as he is in the light, we have fellowship with one another, and the blood of Jesus, his Son, purifies us from all sin' (1 John 1:7). This is an example, like the last one, of an aspect of the saving work of God, healing or cleansing, being perfectly brought together and fulfilled in Jesus.

The Royal Seed

2 Kings 11 relates the incident of a murderous woman, Athaliah, who seeks to wipe out the surviving royal family. Some of the faithful hide Joash, the young prince. He is taken to the Temple where the guards are sworn to protect him and see no blood shed within its precincts. There he is crowned king and Athaliah is put to flight and killed. Joash represents the royal seed, the messianic bloodline linking back to the promise to Eve in Genesis 3:15.

PRAYER

Father, I thank you that Jesus is our wisdom. I thank you for the healing power that flows in his name, and for the cleansing that comes under the cross. Thank you that he is the one to crush the serpent's head and that the enemy could not thwart him. Amen.

MEMORY VERSE

So he went down and dipped himself in the Jordan seven times, as the man of God had told him, and his flesh was restored, and became clean like that of a young boy.   (2 Kings 5:14)

PART THREE –
Jesus in the Wisdom Literature

There are books of poetic sayings, love songs, hymns and long discourses about wisdom or the problem of suffering. Wisdom is the way, a path to peace and blessing. Jesus is the incarnation of wisdom in the New Testament, the lover of our souls, and the only answer to the pain in the world.

Jesus in Job

Job is a poetic, enigmatic book of beautiful prose which explores the question of suffering – particularly, why a righteous man should suffer. There are no slick, easy answers. There are various ideas or details which are seen to point to Jesus:

- The man of sorrows
- The arbitrator
- The ransom
- The redeemer

The Man of Sorrows

There is a story told about a village in France in the nineteenth century. Two teenagers went to see the parish priest, the Curé. They went to confession, one after the other, sitting in the confession box. They peered through the grill at the old priest and played a taunting game with him. They confessed every sin they could imagine, getting more horrendous, daring and pornographic as they went on. Eventually, the priest had had enough. He stepped out of the confessional and took them by the scruff of the neck to the altar. There he got them to kneel down and pointed up to the crucifix, to the image of Jesus hanging on the cross. 'Look at him,' he said. 'Now, tell me that you do not care!' They blushed with embarrassment and slid out of the church, chastened.

You cannot help but be moved by the figure of Job, reduced to pain and misery, depressed in the ash heap. He has lost his children and his home, and now his health. Still, he will not curse God. He wrestles with the questions and ideas of his friends, Eliphaz, Bildad, Zophar and Elihu. They try to work out a theology of suffering ('theodicy' to be technical) but their attempts to pin matters down into a slick, systematic system fall on deaf ears. Job has not sinned, and he does not believe that God is chastising him.

In Job, we see a righteous man filled with suffering, thrown into the crucible of a fallen world. In Jesus we see such a man, the Righteous One, the only sinless man in all history, who became incarnate and embraced the fallen creation. God stepped into the world he had made and was hung on the cross. The Gospels do not give us slick answers to the question of suffering, either, but they do show that God is there in the darkness, alongside us. He has walked where we walk, and perhaps, in one sense, he makes up for making a world where evil could potentially exist by entering it, absorbing sin and suffering on the cross.

The wonderful prophecy of his coming in Isaiah describes him as 'a man of sorrows, and familiar with suffering' (Isaiah 53:3).

The Arbitrator

Job laments:

> He is not a man like me that I might answer him,
> that we might confront each other in court.

If only there were someone to arbitrate between us,
to lay his hand upon us both,
someone to remove God's rod from me,
so that his terror would frighten me no more.
Then I would speak up without fear of him,
but as it now stands with me, I cannot. (Job 9:32–35)

Christians see Jesus as this 'someone', this go-between, the arbitrator between God and humanity. As Paul says: 'For there is one God and one mediator between God and men, the man Christ Jesus, who gave himself as a ransom for all men...' (1 Timothy 2:5–6). By his incarnation, the Son of God stood in our place, walked where we walk, and links heaven and earth.

Chaim Potok in his novel, *My Name is Asher Lev*[1], writes about a young Jewish artist who shocks his friends and family by painting a picture that he feels sums up the suffering of his people. He paints the man on the cross, Jesus. In that figure, he sensed a balance, a symbol of the Creator making up for making a world where pain was possible. Somehow, he was there.

The Ransom

Elihu had this to say:

Yet if there is an angel on his side
as a mediator, one out of a thousand,
to tell a man what is right for him,
to be gracious to him and say,
'Spare him from going down to the pit;

---

1 Chaim Potok, *My Name is Asher Lev*, first edition NY: Alfred A. Knopf, Inc., 1972 (A Borzoi Book).

> I have found a ransom for him' –
>> then his flesh is renewed like a child's;
>>> it is restored as in the days of his youth.
>
> (Job 33:23–25)

Jesus is such a ransom, paying the price for our sin, making up for what it is impossible for us to make up for. Here we tread the mystery of the atonement and all the ideas of propitiation again. Our sins have cost us relationship with the Father but the Son came to take the burden upon himself, to pay a price that we could not pay. These are images and analogies that are limited, difficult, but powerful.

As Jesus said: 'For even the Son of Man did not come to be served, but to serve, and to give his life as a ransom for many' (Mark 10:45).

Job echoes the human condition, the heart cry of humanity for a helper, one who can ransom us from our condition. I have studied world faiths and written about them. They have many insights but they do not have a Saviour. Only Christ is presented as one who meets us where we are to bring us back to God, by grace.

The Redeemer

Job struggles with his faith at times, not surprisingly, but he comes through with a bold confession in God as saviour and in an afterlife:

> I know that my Redeemer lives,
>> and that in the end he will stand upon the earth.
> And after my skin has been destroyed,
>> yet in my flesh I will see God;
> I myself will see him

with my own eyes – I, and not another.
How my heart yearns within me! (Job 19:25–27)

Job's reference to a 'Redeemer' uses the Hebrew term *go'el*, the kinsman-redeemer as in Ruth. This is not a stranger, but one of his kinsmen. This close, familiar sense of God found its fulfilment in Jesus, the incarnation of the Son in an Israelite, one of Job's race. Job also confesses an early belief in the resurrection, a form of afterlife belief that developed gradually through the pages of the Old Testament. Again, in Jesus, we see that hope superbly and supremely.

PRAYER

I thank you, Lord Jesus, that you took flesh and walked where I walk. I thank you that you know my condition, my needs, from the inside. Thank you that you took my place, took up my cause, and brought me before the Father. Thank you that you paid the price for my sin, and I stand in awe and admiration, pouring out gratitude from the bottom of my heart, that you settled what I could never repay. Thank you that you will raise me up and in my risen flesh I will see you one day.

MEMORY VERSE

I know that my Redeemer lives,
 and that in the end he will stand upon the earth.

(Job 19:25)

Jesus in the Psalms

The Psalms are a rich stream of hopes and predictions about Jesus. There are parallel lines of prophetic hope running through the 150 Psalms, split up into five books or collections. This twin line of prediction concerns the Messiah as Son of David and Son of God. There are hopes and beliefs about the anointed one, the king, and glimpses of future glory and of one who embraces suffering. The following ideas are seen as types of Jesus:

- The son or anointed king
- The throne
- The Passion predicted
- The good shepherd
- The rock
- The light
- The redeemer
- The transfigured one
- The priest

The Son or the Anointed King

Western society can be very glib and shallow, celebrity obsessed. Reality shows such as *Big Brother* or magazines that reveal sneaky features and photos of the stars speak to us of a heart's desire to look up to someone, to have values, to serve, to adore. Views of Britney Spears' armpits, or Geri Halliwell's dimples dominate the pages, as well as the severely shrinking waists of pop stars. The God-shaped hole inside us is reflected in the Old Testament role of the king as the anointed servant or son of God.

Many psalms celebrate the role of the king as a servant of God and a sign of his justice. Psalm 2 and Psalm 110 describe the king as God's son. It is a metaphorical title unlike pagan ideas that the ruler was actually a god on earth. The Israelite king had a special authority and calling: 'He said to me, "You are my Son; today I have become your Father"' (Psalm 2:7). Psalm 2 is thought to be a coronation psalm and this celebrates the king's victory. There is a prophetic element when it speaks of his rule and victory over all his enemies:

Ask of me, and I will make the nations your inheritance,
    the ends of the earth your possession.
You will rule them with an iron sceptre;
    you will dash them to pieces like pottery.

(Psalm 2:8–9)

Psalm 110 is enigmatic. It is thought to be a coronation psalm that draws upon very ancient rituals from Jerusalem before King David conquered it, rituals that date back to the time of Melchizedek and beyond. Melchizedek was a priest of El Shaddai and also king of Salem (Genesis 14:18–20). Later Hebrew ideas separated the role of king and priest, and Hebrews reunites them in the person of Christ. He is our high priest and the anointed King.

> The Lord has sworn
>> and will not change his mind:
>> 'You are a priest for ever,
>> in the order of Melchizedek' (Psalm 110:4)

This ancient order was reactivated in the Messiah who united the twin roles from ancient Israel. It was reactivated like ancient seeds re-planted and watered, wonderfully sprouting. And yet there is more than a reinstatement here. There is a fulfilment, something more. The ancient role becomes something greater than was ever imagined, it becomes of universal significance. It speaks of an everlasting Saviour and a salvation that abides. When lost, Jesus is the way and our abiding hope.

Another verse in Psalm 110 gets the commentators talking:

> Arrayed in holy majesty,
>> from the womb of the dawn
>> you will receive the dew of your youth.
>
>> (Psalm 110:3b)

The Jerusalem Bible translates this: 'Royal dignity was yours from the day you were born, on the holy mountains, royal from the womb, from the dawn of your earliest days.'

This refers to Mount Zion and an ancient coronation rite, but the dawn reference is open to interpretation. Does it refer to the infancy of the king, royal from birth (or conception even)? Or is some other ritual involving the dawn involved? We do not know. Augustine of Hippo saw a prediction of Christ here. Taking the verse to mean that the king was born before the dawn, then he took this as a reference to the eternal light of Christ, pre-existing that of the created sun.

Psalm 2 ends with the command to 'Kiss the Son' (Psalm 2:12). This would be an act of homage, kissing the feet of the king as a sign of humility and service. The phrase for 'kiss the son' here is used for worship in the Bible. When we worship Jesus, we kiss the Son, bowing down before him in adoration and gratitude.

The Throne

'… I have sworn to David my servant,
"I will establish your line for ever
     and make your throne firm through all generations."'

(Psalm 89:3–4)

This sacred promise to David fulfils the word given to him through the prophet Nathan (2 Samuel 7). The royal line will continue for ever, as found in the coming of the Messiah. The risen and exalted Jesus will reign for ever. There is a throne that is established in heaven; Christ is risen, he is victorious. I remember meditating upon this passage one day when I sensed a powerful presence of God. I had a picture of this gleaming throne like part of a wave of golden light above and flowing over me. He reigns. For those who are in him, and are washed in his blood, we are under the protection of this throne, covered by its glory. That is a beautiful place to be.

The Passion Predicted

Psalm 22 oozes with the Passion. It was quoted by faithful Jewish martyrs down the ages: 'My God, my God, why

have you forsaken me?' Jesus spoke it out in his final minutes on the cross (see Mark 15:34). Verses 12–18 are an
incredible description of a righteous one suffering the
pains of something like the pains of crucifixion, with enemies surrounding, people gloating, bones out of place and
even 'they have pierced my hands and my feet' (Psalm
2:16b). There is also a reference to casting lots for the suf-
ferer's garments: 'They divide my garments among them
and cast lots for my clothing' (Psalm 2:18). This detail fig-
ures in the Passion narratives in the Gospels. Sometimes,
descriptions of a righteous man suffering (like Job) can be
seen as a type of Christ, but this is far more detailed and
specific.

The Good Shepherd

Psalm 23 describes God as a shepherd who wants to lead
us into peace and blessing, who will be with us in times of
trial and through the 'valley of the shadow of death' –
Jesus is the good shepherd (see John 10:11) and he walks
with us through suffering and death. He tasted the darkness in creation in its fullness, swallowing up death and
rising in triumph (see 1 Corinthians 15:25–27). Our
Creator is not a million miles away, abstract upon a cloud,
unmoved by our human condition. He gets involved; gets
his hands dirty.

The Rock

There are various images about God as a rock in the
Psalms. One girl I once taught thought that this was anything but comforting! 'It makes God sound like a brick...
a lump of rock!' she said. 'How can I pray to that?' The

imagery suggests strength and a place of safety. How I can remember the bliss of standing on terra firma after being rescued from a crumbling hillside by the fire brigade. I was hoisted up to safety and then guided down a sure path. If I had gone any further, the topsoil would have slid away and I would have had nothing to hold onto, hitting the large rocks below. I felt like an idiot, but did I care?

The psalmist can speak of the birds and animals finding safe places in the cliffs or rocks. We, too, can find such a place of refuge:

> For in the day of trouble
>> he will keep me safe in his dwelling;
> he will hide me in the shelter of his tabernacle
>> and set me high upon a rock.
> Then my head will be exalted
>> above the enemies who surround me. (Psalm 27:5–6a)

The image can be about solid ground after the slippery troubles around us:

> ... he set my feet on a rock
> and gave me a firm place to stand. (Psalm 40:2)

In the hidden clefts of the rock there is safety, shelter and food;

> But you would be fed with the finest of wheat;
>> with honey from the rock I would satisfy you.
>>> (Psalm 81:16)

This beautiful image of wild rock honey is suggestive of spiritual blessing and feeding from the heart of Jesus.

Early Christian writers saw a link between the cleft of the rock and the side of Christ. When doubting Thomas was invited to place his hand in the side of Christ (see John 20:27) this was seen as a symbol of salvation, of being in a safe harbour, of being safe 'in Christ', or in the cleft of the rock. The Catholic Church holds Divine Mercy Sunday on the Sunday after Easter, retelling the story of Thomas and seeing forgiveness and mercy streaming forth from the side of Christ on the cross, the stream of blood and water being pictured as red and white light engulfing us.

The Light

God is our light as in Psalm 27:1: 'The Lord is my light and my salvation – whom shall I fear?' Jesus is the light of the world, and our saviour in the flesh.

The Redeemer

God is sometimes hailed as 'Redeemer' in the Psalms such as 19:14:

> May the words of my mouth and the meditation of my
>   heart
>   be pleasing in your sight,
>   O Lord, my Rock and my Redeemer.

God is the *go'el*, the kinsman-redeemer of his people Israel, bound to them through the covenant. God's heart of redemption, the heart that shows he is with his suffering people, breaks open when he takes flesh in Jesus. The early Christians used to draw the Alpha symbol, the shape of a fish, as a secret sign of their faith. This stood for the words

'Jesus Christ, Son of God, Saviour' in Greek, after the Greek for 'fish', 'Ichthus'. 'Saviour' was an early title of Jesus.

The Transfigured One

Solomon's psalm describes his glory and majesty:

> He will endure as long as the sun,
>> as long as the moon, through all generations.
> He will be like rain falling on a mown field,
>> like showers watering the earth.
> In his days the righteous will flourish;
>> prosperity will abound till the moon is no more.
>
> (Psalm 72:5–7)

Jesus, on the mount of transfiguration shone like the sun: 'His face shone like the sun, and his clothes became as white as the light' (Matthew 17:2).

The Priest

Psalm 40 offers a glimpse of the priestly role of the king, a desire to offer himself for the people in the service of God:

> Then I said, 'Here I am. I have come –
>> it is written about me in the scroll.
> I desire to do your will, O my God;
>> your law is within my heart.' (Psalm 40:7–8)

This is quoted in Hebrews as a prediction of the coming of the Son (see Hebrews 10:5–10).

Just before the verses quoted above, the psalmist speaks of sacrifices and sin offerings that God did not desire. He wanted the service and obedience of his servant, an idea that the writer of Hebrews links with the self-offering of Jesus on the cross as the final and eternal sacrifice. As Corrie Ten Boom used to say, when imprisoned in a Nazi concentration camp, 'God is present in the deepest Hell'. His cross went deeper than any human sin and darkness, as the preacher Oswald Chambers used to say.

PRAYER

Father, I praise you that you are King and worthy of all my worship. I bow before you and kiss the Son. I lift up the name of Jesus and thank you for his salvation and all he suffered for me. Hide me in the cleft of the rock, set my feet on a firm place, feed me with the wild honey of your Spirit and guide me through the darkness to your peace. Thank you that you are majestic in holiness, outshining the sun, there before the dawn came into being. Amen.

MEMORY VERSE

... they have pierced all my hands and my feet. I can count all my bones, people stare and gloat over me. They divide my garments among them and cast lots for my clothing. (Psalm 22:16–18)

Jesus in Proverbs

The book of Proverbs is a collection of wise sayings and common sense maxims to guide one through life. A key idea is that wisdom comes from and dwells with God, coming to earth and calling out to humanity. Jesus can be seen in the following aspects:

- Wisdom
- Honey
- The son

Wisdom

Wisdom is personified in Proverbs. She is feminine in form and she calls out to the wise to follow her (see Proverbs 9). Proverbs 8 describes the pre-existent nature of Wisdom:

> The Lord brought me forth as the first of his works,
>   before his deeds of old;
> I was appointed from eternity,
>   from the beginning, before the world began.
> When there were no oceans, I was given birth...
>
> (Proverbs 8:22–24)

This is poetic and suggestive, and a parallel is made with the pre-existence of Christ. This passage is felt behind the background to the prologue to John's Gospel: 'In the beginning was the Word, and the Word was with God, and the Word was God. He was with God in the beginning' (John 1:1).

The Proverbs passage speaks of existence from eternity, but also speaks of being the firstborn of all God's works. The New Testament uses 'birth' imagery in two ways, that of the 'only begotten Son' (see John 3:16) and that of the 'firstborn over all creation' (Colossians 1:15). The former is stretched language, meaning a mysterious, filial relationship within the Godhead that has always existed. The Father is the Father of the Son always. The latter is about the chief, the supreme or the boss. 'Firstborn' can mean this in the ancient world, as the firstborn son was the heir and the superior.

Jesus is described as the wisdom of God several times in the New Testament, as in this moving imagery of Jesus: 'O Jerusalem, Jerusalem, you who kill the prophets and stone those sent to you, how often I have longed to gather your children together, as a hen gathers her chicks under her wings, but you were not willing!' (Luke 13:34).

Jesus compares himself to a mother hen in this beautiful image. Having a feminine symbol for Jesus might sound strange, but this is about caring, life-giving and nurturing. Let us remember that the Holy Spirit has a feminine form in Hebrew, as the brooding, motherly, life-giving force that swept over chaos at the start of creation (Genesis 1:2).

Honey

Honey can be a pleasant experience. The Americans often sweeten their tea and coffee with it. The English tend to spread it on toast and crumpets. Our supermarkets now tend to stock a wide variety of types and nationalities. Various passages in Proverbs speak of wisdom as the sweetness of honey:

> Eat honey, my son, for it is good;
>> honey from the comb is sweet to your taste.
> Know also that wisdom is sweet to your soul;
>> if you find it, there is a future hope for you,
>> and your hope will not be cut off.
>
> (Proverbs 24:13–14)

Jesus is seen as a sweet savour in the New Testament: 'For we are to God the aroma of Christ among those who are being saved and those who are perishing' (2 Corinthians 2:15).

There are various references to tasting the good things of the Lord, too: '… who have shared in the Holy Spirit, who have tasted the goodness of the word of God and the powers of the coming age' (Hebrews 6:4–5).

The Son

An intriguing passage towards the end of Proverbs asks:

> Who has gone up to heaven and come down?
>> Who has gathered up the wind in the hollow of his
>> hands?
> Who has wrapped up the waters in his cloak?
>> Who has established all the ends of the earth?

What is his name, and the name of his son?
    Tell me if you know!   (Proverbs 30:4)

This *crie de coeur* in the face of the mystery of life demands the answer, 'The Lord'. And his son? Only the New Testament has an answer to that – 'Jesus'. Yes, 'son' language is stretched, metaphorical language. A son reveals the nature of the father. Jesus is Son of God in a divine, spiritual sense and not a crudely physical sense, but the sentiment stands. Jesus reveals the true nature of God to us.

PRAYER

I thank you, Father, that Jesus is our wisdom and our guide, our lover, 'mother' and life-giver. Thank you that he has navigated through the currents of sin and death and feeds us with the sweetness of life in the Holy Spirit. Thank you that as your Son he reveals your love to us. Amen.

MEMORY VERSE

Know also that wisdom is sweet to your soul;
    If you find it, there is a future hope for you,
And your hope will not be cut off.   (Proverbs 24:14)

Jesus in Ecclesiastes

Ecclesiastes is a collection of heart-searching, sceptical thoughts and a search for the ways of wisdom. Jesus can be seen in:

- The shaft of light
- The right time
- White garments and anointed heads

The Shaft of Light

After pages of searching, scathing scepticism, there is a glimmer of hope:

Light is sweet,
and it pleases the eyes to see the sun.

(Ecclesiastes 11:7)

This is followed by the sentiment: 'Remember your Creator in the days of your youth...' (Ecclesiastes 12:1). Only God is eternal, and the preacher urges his hearers to seek him before death, before 'the silver cord is severed' or 'the golden bowl is broken' (12:6). Jesus is the light of the world, the light that shines in our darkness (see 2 Corinthians 4:6). It pleases our eyes to see 'the Son', also, the great hope for our lives. When I am dealing with bereaved people at funerals, those who have no or little faith struggle a great deal. Their loss is permanent to them, and this is a heart-rending thing. To have at least a glimmer of hope, underneath the sadness, that you might see the loved one again is a marvel. I once counselled a young person whose friend had been tragically killed in a road accident. She raged against God, declaring that this proved he did not exist. I thought for a moment and then answered quietly, 'No God, no friend.' The existence of form and love in the void of death gives hope. This is not to say that we won't feel pain, anger and loss. We are only human.

The Right Time

Ecclesiastes 3 speaks about the rhythm of the seasons and of life: 'a time to be born and a time to die' and so on. Likewise, God's timing is perfect and has its own rhythm and balance. Galatians 4:4–5a says: 'But when the time had fully come, God sent his Son, born of a woman, born under law, to redeem those under law'. Why Jesus came when he did is a matter of conjecture. Perhaps it was timely that the Roman empire had established a large-scale peace and safety of travel, with trade routes criss-crossing the ancient world and the lingua-franca of Latin or Greek. True, too true, but how much more powerful would it have been if Jesus had come in a world of the Internet and mass media? We do not have those answers. He came when he did and the timing was in God's hands.

Waiting upon the Lord is an important part of spiritual discipline, to be sensitive and within his will. Many are the stories of missionaries and evangelists who feel prompted to go here or there, or speak to this person or that. The timing is just right. Think of Jackie Pullinger, for example, as she describes in *Chasing the Dragon*[1], prayerfully beginning each day before she goes out in the streets of Hong Kong among gangs and addicts. She waits upon God, praying in tongues for fifteen minutes each morning.

White Garments and Anointed Heads

Ecclesiastes 9:8 states: 'Always be clothed in white, and always anoint your head with oil.' This appeal to be clean, cool and sweet-smelling is a type of redemption in Christ. We are to be anointed by the Holy Spirit, a sweet savour to the Lord and cleansed by the blood of Jesus (see 1 John 1:7).

PRAYER
Father, thank you that we can see the light of the Son and find love in our hearts and hope for our spirits. Thank you that you have your times and seasons, and we wait in patience upon your Word and the promptings of your Spirit. Thank you that through the blood of Jesus we stand in purity and are anointed with the blessings of the Holy Spirit as precious oil. Amen.

MEMORY VERSE

Light is sweet,
and it pleases the eyes to see the sun.
(Ecclesiastes 11:7)

---

1 Jackie Pullinger with Andrew Quiche, *Chasing the Dragon*, London: Hodder and Stoughton Ltd, latest issue 2006.

Jesus in the Song of Songs

The Song of Songs is first and foremost a love story. It is erotic love poetry between a lover and his beloved. It is a wooing of the bride by the king. The rabbis also saw it as an allegory of the love of God for the soul, or for Israel. The church sees the bridegroom Christ and his bride, the church. Jesus is:

- The beloved
- The rose and the lily
- The garden of delights

The Beloved

The beloved in the Song is a type of Christ seeking his bride, wooing her, drawing her, seeking communion with her. There is a progression of affection and devotion in the bride from 'My lover is mine and I am his' (2:16) to 'I am my lover's and my lover is mine' (6:3) and then 'I belong to my lover and his desire is for me' (7:10). There is surrender, adoration, longing and belonging to the Lord.

The bride grows in obedience, discipleship and communion with her Lord. This imagery echoes in Ephesians 5:25–27: 'Husbands, love your wives, just as Christ loved the church and gave himself up for her to make her holy, cleansing her by the washing with water through the word, and to present her to himself as a radiant church, without stain or wrinkle or any other blemish, but holy and blameless.'

The beloved also asks to be placed as a seal upon the heart, and has a love as strong as death (Song of Songs 8:6).

Jesus as the beloved, the lover, is the secret to the discipleship and obedience of many. They feel loved, wooed, captivated by love, a love as strong as death that went to the cross. I can think, for example, of a young girl preparing for First Communion from a divorced family. Gradually, through Jesus, she has found deep love, acceptance and forgiveness. When trying an imaginative form of prayer in one of our sessions, she sensed Jesus coming to her, looking her in the eyes and offering her precious food. The exercise was about imagining yourself at a form of the Last Supper. She knew him, his presence, and was moved to tears by the holy love that filled her. It all poured out in the car as her mother picked her up and drove her home.

The Rose and the Lily

Song of Songs 2:1 has the beloved as 'a rose of Sharon, a lily of the valleys'. The symbol of the rose speaks of blood, of sacrifice, and the lily of purity and holiness. Jesus is the sinless Lamb of God. Jesus was the sinless one who could go the cross and make atonement for us. When weighed down by guilt we can know forgiveness. There is a cleansing stream, a fountain filled with blood that atones for us. It is hard to image his perfection in a fallen, imperfect world. When we encounter the Holy we sense the perfection, the awe and the majesty of something way,

way beyond our comprehension. Think, in literary terms, of the first appearance of the Elven folk in Tolkien's 'The Lord of the Rings'. He evokes a sense of the holy and the perfect, the awesome and the cleanly disturbing. In such a presence, Frodo is afraid and attracted at the same time. The Dark Riders run for all they are worth!

The Garden of Delights

The lover enters his garden of delights in Song of Songs 5:1:

> I have come into my garden, my sister, my bride;
> > I have gathered my myrrh with my spice.
> I have eaten my honeycomb and my honey;
> > I have drunk my wine and my milk.

In Near Eastern poetry this is a potent symbol of the consummation of love. Think of the delight of two lovers arm in arm, staring into each other's eyes, tasting their lips. It is a garden of delights. The blessings of the new covenant are pictured as a pleasant perfume or a rich feast: 'The Spirit and the bride say, "Come!" And let him who hears say, "Come!" Whoever is thirsty, let him come; and whoever wishes, let him take the free gift of the water of life' (Revelation 22:17).

PRAYER

Father, I thank you that you seek me out in your love, that Jesus has given all for me as the rose of Sharon and his holiness is as the lily of the valley. I can come into the garden of his delight and eat and drink of his mercy and blessing, covered by his love as a seal upon my heart. I am my beloved's and he is mine. Amen.

MEMORY VERSE

I am my lover's and my lover is mine.

(Song of Songs 6:3)

PART FOUR –
Jesus in the Prophets

The Prophets take up much of the Old Testament Scriptures. They span a few hundred years and often speak about concerns of their day, telling forth the word of God to their generation. Naturally, principles and revelations about God's nature are true for all ages and we can drink from these excellent pools of spiritual insight. There are also future predictions, glimpses and hopes of things to come. In the Prophets, we find many oracles about the coming Messiah, as well as some other types or symbols that are suggestive of Jesus. Also, in the Prophets there are precious moments, revelations of the nature and names of God. These insights into his heart are fulfilled in the life of Jesus: 'No-one has ever seen God, but God the One and Only, who is at the Father's side, has made him known' (John 1:18).

Jesus in Isaiah

Isaiah falls into three sections from 1–39, 40–54, and 55–66. Leaving aside the question of whether all of the book is by Isaiah or later sections were added by his disciples, there is a bold sweep of divine revelation and oracular stirrings. Augustine advised new converts to read this book first in the Old Testament after devouring the Gospels. It is full of the gospel. Isaiah had had a blistering vision of the glory of God at the start of his ministry and there is a cutting edge all through the work. Jesus can seen as:

- The promised child
- The servant
- The coming one

The Promised Child

A series of oracles in the first part of Isaiah concern a coming child, a holy child who will bring blessing to his people.

Isaiah 7:14: 'Therefore the Lord himself will give you a sign: The virgin will be with child and will give birth to a son, and will call him Immanuel.'

The oracle about the virgin birth had no precedent in

the Old Testament and stands alone in this passage. This was taken up by Matthew and Luke and seen as being fulfilled in the birth of Jesus. Some critical scholars argue that the word for 'virgin' is more neutral meaning 'maiden' or 'young woman'. They think the virgin birth is just a legend, a misunderstanding of this ancient passage. However, closer attention suggests that the Hebrew term should be translated according to context. The Greek version used a word commonly meaning 'virgin', and the evangelists clearly understood this in the same way.

Isaiah 9:6: 'For to us a child is born, to us a son is given, and the government will be on his shoulders. And he will be called Wonderful Counsellor, Mighty God, Everlasting Father, Prince of Peace.'

This striking array of titles tells us that this is to be no ordinary child. There are claims of divinity and divine authority upon him. 'Everlasting Father' links up with the earlier 'Immanuel', i.e. 'God is always with us'. 'Prince of Peace' is a reminder of Melchizedek, the king of Salem (meaning 'Peace'). Maybe some of the earlier, antiquarian rituals and titles from the pre-Davidic Jerusalem are on offer here, or they are totally new revelations. Whatever, Jesus fulfilled them superbly.

Isaiah 11:1–10, which begins: 'A shoot will come up from the stump of Jesse; from its roots a Branch will bear fruit.' Blessing and renewal comes to the world, with the wolf living with the lamb. The shoot and root imagery echoes that of the risen Jesus in Revelation 22:16: 'I am the Root and the Offspring of David, and the bright Morning Star.'

This enigmatic, paradoxical image of the root and branch is the stuff of deep 'myth' in the sense that a

Tolkien would use it, deep roots of the saga and predictive hopes from the dawn of time to seal the blessings of the future. He was a practising Roman Catholic, steeped in the Scriptures (and involved in the English translation of the Jerusalem Bible). No wonder he told great, inspiring, epic tales. And the beauty is that the Bible story is graced with history; it happened and will come to pass.

I recently heard a preacher lamenting the Christmas decorations in churches and the obsession with the infant Jesus. It reminded him of his mother, now deceased, who used to show all his friends an old photo album. This had beloved pictures of him as a baby and young boy, much to his cringing embarrassment. He wondered if the Lord felt the same way; we deal with Jesus as the grown up man, the saviour now, and not the child.

I can sympathize with the idea of rejecting overly sentimental images of Jesus, the gentle child, full of 'ahs' and 'coos' as people pile into church once a year and that's it. But there is something more to the child in the manger tradition that reminds us of the oracles of Isaiah, the wonder of the incarnation and his humility. Almighty God put himself into our hands, into Mary's hands, and was laid in the straw. My bishop recently made the local newspaper by advising his clergy to shock Christmas congregations by bringing a bucket of manure into church and tipping it over a sheet by the crib. 'That should bring the reality home!' he smiled.

There is a rich and wondrous tradition of the holy babe in Catholicism, in the arms of the Madonna, seen in visions in places such as Prague or by holy saints like Anthony of Padua. It might seem a little strange and alien, but it echoes the wonder of the incarnation, never to be forgotten.

The Servant

The middle section of Isaiah deals with oracles concerning an anonymous servant of the Lord who will bring blessings and will offer himself as an atonement for sin. This reminds us that Jesus has a servant heart who will bend down and wash the feet of his diciples, causing uproar and shock in their social circles. This was only done by the servant of the house, the most menial person to honour the guests. Jesus is also the Servant who came down to give his life for us:

> Who being in the very nature of God did not consider equality with God something to be grasped but made himself nothing, taking the very nature of a servant, being found in human likeness. And being found in appearance as a man he humbled himself and became obedient to death – even death on a cross. (Philippians 2:6–8)

I recall reading the testimony of the chair of the G.K. Chesterton society (he of 'Father Brown' fame), Stratford Caldecott, who has also written about the beautiful Christian imagery in Tolkien's *The Lord of the Rings* in his book, *Secret Fire*. Stratford was a bohemian seeker after truth, loving imaginative science fiction and esoteric, eastern faiths who sought enlightenment. He tried this meditation technique and philosophy, only to feel rather empty. These ways might have had insights about the nature of the world and the human soul, but they had no answers. When he drifted into a church, through his wife, he saw something different. The centre of the Christian faith was about incarnation, about God made man, Christ the Servant stooping low to find us where we are. Eastern faiths were all about enlightenment, Christianity about redemption. In the enigmatic references to the Servant in Isaiah, we catch something of the face of Christ to come.

Isaiah 42:1–9: This figure will be merciful and pastoral, a shepherd as well as a ruler. 'A bruised reed he will not break, and a smouldering wick he will not snuff out' (42:3). Here we see Jesus touching the leper, forgiving the prostitutes and embracing the tax collectors. The servant will be able 'to open eyes that are blind, to free captives from prison and to release from the dungeon those who sit in darkness' (42:7).

Isaiah 49:1–7: Here, the servant is to be a 'light for the Gentiles' (49:6) and the one who was abhorred will be raised up, bowed down to by kings and princes (49:7). In this servant passage he is identified with Israel. There is a sense in which the nation, the people of Israel, are all the servant of the Lord, inheritors of his promises. However, as the 'servant songs' develop, there is a focus, a narrowing down to one special Israelite.

Isaiah 52:13–53:1–12: This amazing passage deals with the servant who will be despised, beaten, abused, rejected but will be an offering, an atonement for the sins of the people. This was new to the Old Testament. They were used to sin offerings to be sure, but of animals. That a person, a prophet or a ruler would so offer himself was strange, pagan-sounding even: 'But he was pierced for our transgressions, he was crushed for our iniquities; the punishment that brought us peace was upon him, and by his wounds we are healed' (53:5).

The servant is even compared to the scapegoat from Leviticus:

> We all, like sheep, have gone astray,
>   each of us has turned to his own way;
> and the Lord has laid on him
>   the iniquity of us all. (53:6)

The passage then states that the servant will stand before his accusers silently, not saying a word – as did Jesus before the Sanhedrin. He was given a grave with the rich, as was Jesus when Joseph of Arimathea gave up his tomb. There is hope at the end:

> After the suffering of his soul,
>   he will see the light of life and be satisfied. (53:11a)

A hint of resurrection?

This passage stands out in the whole of the Old Testament. Jesus referred to this when he told his disciples that it was written that the Son of man must suffer (see Luke 18:31–34). I remember studying this passage in my university course, wading through monographs and books that examined every possible contender for the identity of the servant from the time of Isaiah. No one fitted – no one. It is an enigma. Today, the rabbis interpret this as applying to the people of Israel and avoid any messianic interpretations because of the Christians. Only one man in history fits the bill, though. Jesus of Nazareth. Take heart that through the death of this man there is forgiveness and peace. When weighed down by guilt or feeling a failure, this is the one we can turn to. I remember arguing and protesting when I first heard the message of the cross. I argued, 'How can the death of this one man 2,000 years ago save me today?' But if this one man among many was unique, if he was God made man, then his death makes all the difference all through time.

The Coming One

The prophecy draws to a close with a vision of Glory, the glory of God reprised and coming to earth. Anyone who has felt a touch of the Glory, of the Presence of the Lord, will wonder at this. It is a holy heaviness, something that makes you sink to your knees or fall flat on your face. In this holy presence are healing and joy, tears and laughter. One passage wonders:

Who is this coming from Edom,
    from Bozrah, with his garments stained crimson?
Who is this, robed in splendour,
    striding forward in the greatness of his strength.
'It is I, speaking in righteousness, mighty to save.'
                                  (Isaiah 63:1)

The coming one, the one who will bring the kingdom and the glory, has his robes stained red. Reading on, this is from treading the winepress of judgment. The image is suggestive, though, of Jesus, the lamb who was slain, reigning in glory:

Worthy is the Lamb, who was slain,
to receive power and wealth and wisdom and strength
and honour and glory and praise!   (Revelation 5:12)

PRAYER

Father, I praise you for the coming of the Christ-child, for his incarnation and humility. Thank you for the grace and salvation that flowed from him. Thank you that he was your servant who opens the eyes of the blind, rescues us from darkness, touches us with mercy and is a light to the nations. Thank you that he has stained his robes red with his own blood, making peace between us. Amen.

MEMORY VERSE

But he was pierced for our transgressions, he was crushed for our infirmities, the punishment that brought us peace was upon him, and by his wounds we are healed.   (Isaiah 53:5)

Jesus in Jeremiah and Lamentations

Jeremiah was a prophet at the time of the rise of Babylon and he saw Judah and the people of Jerusalem go into exile. They would not heed his warnings and would not repent. Much of the book is for the people of the time, but there is an oracle which speaks of Jesus. Lamentations is a lament, a series of poetic refrains weeping over the fall of Jerusalem. Jesus is seen as:

- The spring of living water
- The healer
- The righteous branch
- The one who lamented

The Spring of Living Water

Jeremiah 2:13 complains: '... they have forsaken me, the spring of living water, and have dug their own cisterns...' Here, the Lord is as a spring of living water, a fountain of life. Jesus is such in John 4 when he tells the Samaritan woman that streams of living water will well up within her. Flowing water suggests cleanliness, purity and life. In a small village near to my parish in West Sussex there is an ancient spring known as St Mary's Spring. There are suggestions that this had been the focus of a pilgrimage in the Middle Ages and there are a surprising number of parish churches dedicated to the Virgin within the area, including my own. Now, it is an old iron pipe, slightly bricked in, that spouts a clean, refreshing stream of water that never stops, even when the water levels are low. What stories and legends were associated with this we do not know, but many springs and holy wells had been sacred sites in pagan times as signs of life. If there was no local saint, then these became Mary's by default after the conversion of England. The water was a symbol of the living water given by Jesus, poured forth from Mary in the incarnation. A small wooden figurine I have of Mary has her holding out the Christ child for all the world to embrace, rather than cradling him to her breast as you normally see. It is as though he is flowing out to all the world. He is the giver of Living Water, the one who brings the gift of the Holy Spirit. This is the man who can refresh our souls, just as a cupful of that spring water quenches physical thirst in a hot summer.

The Healer

There is a lament in Jeremiah 8:22:

> Is there no balm in Gilead?
>   Is there no physician there?
> Why then is there no healing
>   for the wound of my people?

This heart cry is answered in Jesus the saviour and healer who atones for sin and heals the soul. The Lord is also called 'Redeemer' in Jeremiah 50:34:

> Yet their Redeemer is strong;
>   the Lord Almighty is his name.

This was also wonderfully fulfilled in the Word made flesh. Healing is a mystery. We cannot make it happen or work out magical formulas to drum up faith. All we can do is trust, be open, soak in the promises of Scripture and humbly invite prayer. I have known healings in our parish. My wife was healed of fibromyalgia so simply, suddenly and unemotionally. This was such a release and a delight. She had not been able to bend properly, to sleep properly for months and she never knew which bit of her would hurt the next day. I have seen a woman who had surgery for throat cancer be able to speak again and to swallow, gulping down her drinks when she was told that there was little hope of such things. I have a young mother in the parish who was suffering from sciatica when heavily pregnant. Simply meditating upon some healing Scriptures brought release as the power of the Word seeped into her spirit and this somehow, wonderfully, affected her body. I have seen an elderly man, who should have died nearly two years before, given measures of healing from various crippling cancers and his quality of life has dramatically improved. These are wonderful things, but many are not healed in such a way, though they do feel a peace, a holy touch, through the healing prayer ministry.

The Righteous Branch

Jeremiah 23:5 reads: ' "The days are coming," declares the
Lord, "when I will raise up to David a righteous Branch, a
King who will reign wisely and do what is just and right in
the land." '

This is similar to Isaiah's oracle about the shoot from
the stump of Jesse, the hope of a restored monarchy and
a reign of peace and righteousness after the fall of
Jerusalem and the deportation (and death) of the reigning
king and his princes. There is one who is to come, a messiah. Linked with the theme of kingship is the description
of God as a shepherd who will watch over his flock
(Jeremiah 31:10) and another David will be raised up
(Jeremiah 30:9). Out of despair and death will come hope.
God is a God of resurrection. If you are feeling that you
are in a blind alley, a spiritual dead end, then take courage
and look up.

The One who Lamented

Lamentations reminds us of the time when Jesus
lamented over Jerusalem:

O Jerusalem, Jerusalem, you who kill the prophets and
stone those sent to you, how often I have longed to gather
your children together, as a hen gathers her chicks under
her wings, but you were not willing.   (Luke 13:34)

My friend, Canon Andrew White of the Foundation of
Reconciliation in the Middle East, speaks of the pain of
the peacemaker, of the tears that have to be shed. This
larger than life, amiable, compassionate priest has seen

failure and hatred, and at one time four of his lay workers at the Anglican Church in Baghdad were killed. He was also a friend of the American peaceworker, Tom Fox, who was kidnapped and found shot. He had urged him to leave Iraq for his own safety, and had sent teams out to negotiate for him and his colleagues. One negotiator went missing. All of these dear friends' bodies were never found.

Perhaps also in Jeremiah we see a suffering servant, a righteous prophet who is abused and rejected, a 'man of sorrows'.

PRAYER

Thank you, Father, that Jesus is the righteous Branch of David who reigns over us, the healer and redeemer to whom every knee shall bow and every tongue confess that he is Lord. Thank you, too, for his mercy and compassion. Amen.

MEMORY VERSE

Yet their Redeemer is strong;
   the Lord Almighty is his name.   (Jeremiah 50:34)

Jesus in Ezekiel

Ezekiel was another prophet at the time of the Babylonian invasion and the exile. He saw the glory depart from the Temple and knew that doom was at hand. If we compare the prophets to modern musicians or rock stars, then whilst Jeremiah might be a righteous, blues-singing Bono, or Isaiah an imaginative, oracular Bowiesque figure, then Ezekiel would be more surreal – perhaps Freddie Mercury singing 'Bohemian Rhapsody'. His visions were wilder, more colourful and heavily laden with symbols. I am playing with words here, and mean no disrespect, of course. Within this dramatic figure's visions, there are seen some glimpses of Jesus:

- The figure in the glory
- The wheel within a wheel
- The good shepherd
- The Temple and the river

The Figure in the Glory

In amongst a vision of wings and light, or lightning and wheels, of living creatures and bronze, there was a figure, a form of a man:

I saw that from what appeared to be his waist up he looked like glowing metal, as if full of fire, and... brilliant light surrounded him. Like the appearance of a rainbow in the clouds on a rainy day, so was the radiance around him. This was the appearance of... the glory of the Lord. When I saw it, I fell face down, and I heard the voice of one speaking. (Ezekiel 1:27–28)

Ezekiel saw the Glory, the Skekinah, the Presence. He fell face down, as people do when God manifests in this way. When approaching his tomb in Iraq the locals insist that you take off your shoes, even when driving your car. This is the eastern custom when stepping on holy ground, just as they take their shoes off in the mosques. There are small alcoves around the tomb where people sit all night to sense the coming of the Glory of the Lord and there they seek healing. God's presence was upon this ancient prophet so mightily that something of it still lingers upon this earth.

In the prophecy, the figure of the man is suggestive of the pre-existent Christ, as with the earlier passages of the Angel of the Lord. It also echoes the splendid vision of the risen Jesus at the beginning of Revelation. 'His head and hair were white like wool, as white as snow, and his eyes were like blazing fire. His feet were like bronze glowing in a furnace...' (Revelation 1:14–15).

The Wheel within a Wheel

Part of the curious details of the vision at the start of Ezekiel's ministry is that the wheels on the structure interlock; there are wheels within wheels: '... Each appeared to be made like a wheel intersecting a wheel' (Ezekiel 1:16).

Some have seen in this a coded reference to the incarnation, of the joining of the two natures of God and man in Jesus.

The Good Shepherd

Ezekiel 34 predicts the coming of Jesus, the good shepherd, as God promises to raise up a new shepherd and care for his people: 'As a shepherd looks after his scattered flock when he is with them, so will I look after my sheep' (Ezekiel 34:12a).

Here we see the servant heart of Jesus again, for the good shepherd lays down his life for the sheep. In Eastern sheep pens, the shepherd sleeps above the door to defend the flock from robbers and predators. Hired hands would probably run, but the owner of the sheep will risk his life for them.

The Temple and the River

Ezekiel concerns himself with a prediction of the new covenant of the Spirit (Ezekiel 36) and then goes on to describe the new Temple, the glorious, restored, final Temple after the old one had been destroyed. From this a sacred river of life flows in Ezekiel 47. He wades out into it until it is so deep that he has to swim in it. The river is a symbol of the gift of the Holy Spirit, poured out on all flesh. The new Temple is Jesus himself, the atoning, risen Lord: 'On the last and greatest day of the Feast, Jesus stood and said in a loud voice, "If anyone is thirsty, let him come to me and drink. Whoever believes in me, as the Scripture has said, streams of living water will flow from within him." By this he meant the Spirit, whom those who believed in him were later to receive' (John 7:37–39a).

I remember watching an old TV series called *Survival*, a nature programme. One sticks in my mind about the life that returned, almost miraculously, to a desert region when the spring rains came each year. Seeds sprouted again and animals returned. Fish swam in the rivers again. It was verdant, teeming, alive. How like the gift of the Holy Spirit this is, bringing life and refreshment where there was doubt, struggle and guilt before.

There are similar images of blessing found elsewhere, such as Isaiah 44:3–5, where the Lord promises to pour out his Spirit like streams on dry ground. Ezekiel is more focused and messianic in his vision of this, though.

PRAYER

I thank you, Lord, for your glory, and I bow in adoration before you. I thank you that Jesus came and lived among us and burst out into Glory again, leading many sons and daughters into that light and joy. Thank you that from his body comes salvation and blessing, the gift of the life-giving Spirit within us. Amen.

MEMORY VERSE

This was the appearance of the glory of the Lord. When I saw it, I fell face down, and I heard the voice of one speaking.   (Ezekiel 1:27–28)

Jesus in Daniel

Daniel is set in the exile in Babylon and then under the kings of Persia when Babylon fell. The latter part of the book is composed of vivid, symbolic imagery called 'apocalyptic'. People debate how old this style is, but it flourished with a vengeance between the Testaments. Still, this section of Daniel might be much older. Jesus can be seen in three ways:

- The rock
- The one like a son of man
- The son of man

The Rock

In Daniel 2, Nebuchadnezzar has a dream of a giant made of different metals, representing the various kingdoms of Babylon, Persia, the Greeks and Rome. Finally a rock strikes the feet and topples the statue. The rock is Jesus bringing the kingdom of God. This speaks of victory, the resurrection being a pledge of this. God's way will win out and justice will be done. Survivors of the genocide in Rwanda know this pain and hope. That love could blossom again or peace walk the streets in that blood-soaked land is a miracle. This was a horrible and extreme situation as people were called 'cockroaches' and hunted down as vermin. Despair hit apartheid South Africa, too. I remember a friend of mine who had been a priest under Bishop Desmond Tutu, working in Zululand. He worked in a parish close to me in England for a time and told me many stories of his days over there. He had seen his fair share of violence, even being shot in the stomach as someone tried to steal his car. His humour and openness were infectious, asking me where you could buy the drugs to vaccinate your cat, as they had to do this in Zululand as the vets were so far away. He kept hordes of chickens in his rectory just as in Africa, but the noise of the cockrel was too much for the commuting professionals around him! Yes, he had seen too many things in South Africa and he helped on the Truth and Reconciliation forums. He spoke movingly once about a young white man, orphaned, who had worked for the security forces and had killed a black youth. He confessed this and the boy's mother stood up and confronted him. After a tense moment she said, 'The Lord has helped me forgive you. From today you will be my son!' You cannot imagine how someone can have a change of heart to do this. These incidents are glimmers of hope, hints of resurrection. When we are feeling down and rejected by others, God cares. The Holy Spirit convicts but never condemns (see Romans 8:1), and he always comes with grace.

The One Like a Son of Man

Daniel 3 tells the story of the crazy decree of Nebuchadnezzar that everyone should worship a golden image of himself. Three Jews, Shadrach, Meshach and Abednego, are thrown into a blazing furnace as they refuse to bow down. They are unharmed, protected by a supernatural presence. The onlookers report a fourth man in the flames. Was he an angel of the Lord or the pre-existent Christ? He is described as 'one like a son of man', meaning a human being. Some do testify to miraculous deliverances in difficult spots. Many stories abound of angelic encounters such as the girl who stopped at a gas station in a section of the US she did not know, feeling compelled by the Holy Spirit. There a mechanic told her she needed to find the local hospital and gave her directions. She went to drive away and the man had vanished. She saw that the gas station was closed, all along! At the hospital she had barely approached reception when she collapsed with a life threatening condition that she had no idea that she was suffering from. The medics reached her just in time and her life was spared.

The Son of Man

Daniel 7 contains a vision of four beasts and then the coming of a human being who defeats them and reigns over them, sent from God:

> In my vision at night I looked, and there before me was one like a son of man, coming with the clouds of heaven. He approached the Ancient of Days and was led into his presence. He was given authority, glory and sovereign power; all peoples, nations and men of every language worshipped him. (Daniel 7:13–14a)

This was a prediction of the Messiah, one from heaven who was worshipped as God. This was an unusual image for a Jewish prophet for whom only the Lord was to be worshipped. Clearly, the Son of man was linked to the divine. Interestingly, there is no known, definite use of this title for the Messiah before the Gospels. (Of course, some old texts might one day be unearthed that shows that it was so used.) Jesus used it freely in the Gospels, possibly as a neutral title that he could fill with his own meaning, as it did not have much coinage at the time. 'Messiah' was politically explosive as people thought that such a figure would rise up and fight the Romans.

Jesus uses the Son of man imagery in his own end-time teaching: 'At that time men will see the Son of Man coming in clouds with great power and glory' (Mark 13:26).

God became man, the Creator stepped into his creation. That is the message of the vision of the Son of Man in Daniel. God reached out to us on our level in an act of incredible, universe silencing humility. There is a children's book about a mouse that wants to reach up and kiss its friend the giraffe. The mouse tries and tries and tries to climb higher and higher and higher. He stands on a pea, on a cabbage, on a cup and many other items. Then he teeters on the top of this wobbling tower and falls head over heels to the ground. Then the giraffe looks at him, lowers his long neck and kisses the little mouse. That is such a beautiful symbol of the dynamic of the incarnation, God reaching down to us where we are. Of all the religions of the world only Christianity has a redeemer.

PRAYER

Father, I praise you that Jesus is the rock of our salvation and his is an everlasting kingdom. I thank you that he rescues us from the power of sin and is the one who comes on the clouds to bring in the kingdom. I look forward to his coming and say, *'Maranatha!'*, 'Come, Lord!' Amen.

MEMORY VERSE

In the time of those kings, the God of heaven will set up a kingdom that will never be destroyed, nor will it be left to another people. It will crush all those kingdoms, and bring them to an end, but it will itself endure for ever.   (Daniel 2:44)

Jesus in Hosea

Hosea was a prophet in the northern kingdom of Israel in the eighth century BC, calling the people back to the Lord before the fall of their capital, Samaria.

Jesus is seen in this book as:

- The forgiving bridegroom
- Rising on the third day
- Called out of Egypt
- Lifting the yoke and bending low

The Forgiving Bridegroom

Hosea the prophet is told to marry a harlot, a faithless wife. She runs off, plays the adulteress, and he seeks after her, bringing her home. This is an acted parable of God's love for Israel and her faithlessness to him. Jesus is the bridegroom who seeks out his people, washing them and forgiving them by his blood. Thus Jesus calls the Magdalene who washed his feet with her tears, diminutive Zacchaeus and many others in the Gospels. He is the good shepherd who seeks out the lost sheep.

Many are the cases I have known of a wife or a husband who has an unbelieving partner. There can be tensions and conflicts. Perhaps the believer is prohibited from going to church for a time, surviving on personal prayer, Bible reading, books and tapes. Perhaps there is mockery or jealousy. I remember a gentle man whose wife threw a Bible at him when he got up to go to church on a Sunday. She was angry and jealous, afraid that something else was taking his attention. Her loved her, patiently and faithfully, until her heart melted. This is a little like Hosea with Gomer.

Jesus came to call all the lost sheep including each one of us. What might he find in our hearts that is unfaithful to him? And yet he still loves us.

Rising on the Third Day

The people seek to return to the Lord and hope by the third day he will have healed them and raised them up:

> After two days he will revive us;
>> on the third day he will restore us,
>> that we may live in his presence. (Hosea 6:2)

The theme of 'the third day' recurs in the Old Testament in various places. This can be seen as a type of the resurrection of Jesus, on the third day after his crucifixion. There seem to be times and seasons of the Spirit, a right moment for action, for deliverance or healing. We are called to be patient and faithful even when we do not feel like it or when God does not seem to be around.

Called out of Egypt

'When Israel was a child, I loved him, and out of Egypt I called my son' (Hosea 11:1). This text was quoted by Matthew as a prediction of the descent into Egypt by the holy family (Matthew 2:13–15). Of course, it was also a reference backwards in time to the Exodus as the people of God were called out slavery. It is one of those happy coincidences that the rabbis looked for when seeking to interpret the Bible for their own day. It is worth reflecting on how the family of Jesus went through suffering. They lived as asylum seekers, fleeing persecution. We do not know what kin Joseph had in Jewish settlements in Egypt. There were many Jews there, particularly in Alexandria. Where they stayed and how he earned a living we do not know. It might not have been the radical, frightened act of a desperate refugee today, having nothing but the clothes they are standing up in and knowing no one. Still, it cost them, and they had to live with fear and separation from their home for a time. It is easy to look at Christmas scenes and cribs and feel a warm, holy glow. They were living in dangerous times, and were very much in touch with reality. The child who was born in a stable among the straw and cattle was off on a trek to a foreign land pretty sharpish.

Lifting the Yoke and Bending Low

Hosea 11 also has a moving passage about God's care for Israel as he brought them out of Egypt and through the wilderness: 'I led them with cords of human kindness, with ties of love; I lifted the yoke from their neck and bent down to feed them' (Hosea 11:4).

Lifting the yoke reminds us of Jesus saying, 'Take my yoke upon you' in Matthew 11:29. Bending low is an image of the incarnation as God comes down to meet us where we are. In fact, Hosea shows us a sense of God as passionate about his people, trying to be involved in their lives and history. The God of Israel was not remote, abstract on a cloud a million miles away.

The other wonderful thing is that the yoke is bespoke. It does not chaff or scar. It is just the right size. I remember a dream I once had of Vivienne Westwood descending a flight of stairs in a crowded Christian assembly! Jesus appeared beside her as people drew back in surprise. Such an enigmatic, flamboyant, anarchic figure was not expected in a Christian convention. There were gasps as Jesus put his arm on her shoulder and walked beside her. Then, as these things can only happen in dreams, I took the place of the colourful fashion designer and felt the powerful, intimate love of God around me. This touched me deeply as I was feeling rather misunderstood and out of place there. He knows us better than we know ourselves. The yoke is always bespoke.

PRAYER

I thank you, Lord, for your faithfulness to me when I fail you. I thank you for Jesus dying for me, showing his unending love. I thank you that I was called out of 'Egypt' to the glorious liberty of the children of God and that I am raised up in heavenly places with Jesus. Amen.

MEMORY VERSE

I led them with cords of human kindness, with ties of love; I lifted the yoke from their neck and bent down to feed them. (Hosea 11:4)

Jesus in Joel

Joel is a short book written after a plague of locusts
has attacked the people. He calls them to repentance.
Jesus is prefigured as:

* The restorer
* The baptizer with the Holy Spirit

The Restorer

Joel promises restoration after a time of repentance: 'I will
repay you for the years the locusts have eaten...' (Joel
2:25).

The work of the heavenly restorer is part of salvation,
of making whole. The Greek verb *sozo* for 'save' means to
heal and to be whole, also. The beauty of a restored relationship with God when a person comes to faith and new
birth is a wonderful thing. Their spirits are whole and
something new has come into their life, no matter what
hurts and let downs there have been along the way. I knew
someone who had had a traumatic, fearful adolescence
and when he came to faith he sensed the still, small voice
of God telling him, 'All that you missed out in your
teenage years will be more than made up to you in the
new birth.'

My contact with post-abortion counselling has opened

my eyes to the work of the Restorer. I can think of one young woman who struggled through a healing retreat and found great release and forgiveness. Later she wrote to me about the anger and guilt that were surfacing about another abortion she had had. She would have to work through these buried emotions, too, on the foundation of the work that God was already doing. Jesus is in the restoration business. His sensitive touch to lepers and the healing of the blind beggars shows this compassion. The incident in John 9:6–7 when Jesus mixed mud and saliva and healed the blind man suggests restoration, the work of a heavenly sculptor or divine creator, forming life from the clay.

The Baptizer with the Holy Spirit

And afterwards,
   I will pour out my Spirit on all people.
Your sons and daughters will prophesy,
   your old men will dream dreams,
   your young men will see visions. (Joel 2:28)

The apostle Peter referred to this verse on the day of Pentecost. What had happened to them was a fulfilment of that ancient promise after Jesus had died, risen and returned to the Father. Jesus is the baptizer with the Holy Spirit. John the Baptist also referred to him in this way: 'He will baptise you with the Holy Spirit and with fire' (Matthew 3:11b).

When the Azusa Street revival broke out in Los Angeles in 1906, William Seymour, the one-eyed, shy black preacher lay with his face in a show box, seeking God. As the fire of the Spirit fell, a motley crowd assembled of varying race, social background, denomination and age. The meetings were in an old warehouse and people sat on the floor, oblivious to the lack of comfort, seeking the blessing of God. The Spirit is no respecter of persons. He delights to unite and live in different people as his temple. This radical, unifying, levelling experience is the beauty of the charismatic renewal.

PRAYER

Father, I thank you for the outpouring of the Holy Spirit in my life that I have done nothing to deserve. Thank you that Jesus has brought this gift by his grace. Amen.

MEMORY VERSE

I will repay you for the years the locusts have eaten...

(Joel 2:25)

Jesus in Amos

Amos prophesied at the same time as Hosea in eighth century Judea. He lamented the lack of justice in the land. Jesus is seen in:

- The righteous one who brings justice
- The restored tent of David

The Righteous One Who brings Justice

Jesus is the faithful Israelite who perfectly fulfilled the Law. The heart cry of the Lord through Amos for justice was answered in the man from Nazareth. Today our world cries out for justice, too, as many struggle to find decent food or health care in the developing world. A friend of mine recently returned from a trip to South Africa to stay with the family of a Zulu girl whom they had given extended hospitality to in the UK. The Zulu woman was lively, with infectious laughter that filled a whole room. My friend saw much beauty in a land of contrasts. The girl's family were rich in love and family loyalty, but they were materially poor. She reflected how in the West we can seem to have so much but we are poor emotionally and spiritually. Then there was grinding poverty alongside extreme affluence, with people dying of AIDS gathered in huts as expensive hospitals stood down the road. People did not seem to notice or care. This was hard for her, very hard. The Spirit groans within us (Romans 8:23, 26) as we await the coming of the kingdom in all its fullness.

The Restored Tent of David

'In that day I will restore David's fallen tent' (Amos 9:11a). Amos begins to speak about a coming Day of the Lord. This is not yet Messianic in this book, though other scriptures make it plain that only he can bring it about. The reference to the fallen tent of David is about restoring the tabernacle before the Temple was built. The old days had real worship with faithful people; now there are empty rites and there is much hypocrisy. Jesus is the true tabernacle of David (John 1:14) and this tent will never fall again. Many in the churches today sense that there is an outpouring of the Holy Spirit to raise up new, heartfelt, free praise with manifestations and gifts of the Holy Spirit. I have been present in such gatherings where you sense the holiness of God. The hairs on the back of your neck can stand on end as the assembly sings in tongues. People sometimes sense the singing of the angels mixed in with this or even feel their presence. I have felt this on a couple of occasions, sensing them hovering above and around the assembly. Once they were to my right and once above the chancel arch in our parish church. I tend to sense these things in monochrome, somehow. It is hard to explain. Maybe I just don't tune in with my spiritual eyes very well, but it is a very holy and wholesome experience. Praise is rising up from many hearts of different backgrounds and denominations.

PRAYER

Father, I thank you that Jesus is the Holy One, the Just One who justifies us before you by grace. Thank you that he is the living tabernacle, the true centre of worship, a light that can never be extinguished. Amen.

MEMORY VERSE

But let justice roll on like a river, righteousness like a never-failing stream! (Amos 5:24)

Jesus in Obadiah

Obadiah prophesied again the nation of Edom as they had not come to Israel's aid when invaded. Jesus is seen in the role of:

- The deliverer

The Deliverer

But on Mount Zion will be deliverance;
it will be holy,
and the house of Jacob
will possess its inheritance. (Obadiah 17)

Jesus is our deliverer, and in him all these hopes have come to pass: 'For he must reign until he has put all his enemies under his feet' (1 Corinthians 15:25); '...to wait for his Son from heaven, whom he raised from the dead – Jesus, who rescues us from the coming wrath' (1 Thessalonians 1:10); 'For he has rescued us from the dominion of darkness and brought us into the kingdom of the Son he loves, in whom we have redemption, the forgiveness of sins' (Colossians 1:13–14).

Those who go through great persecution are often given touches of grace to encourage and assure them of the coming deliverance of God. There was the Russian solider, Vanya, for example, who was imprisoned in a Gulag and badly treated for his Baptist faith. When struggling with the severe cold – he was made to stand outside sometimes naked – he was granted a vision of heaven as an angel escorted him. He saw glory, luscious grass and life. One small detail that sticks in my mind is the urging of the angel to follow through the grass. When Vanya hesitated, afraid of snakes, he was told, 'There are no snakes here.' Or I can think of the Chinese Brother Yun, nicknamed 'the Heavenly Man', who was badly beaten and mocked for his faith in a Chinese prison. He heard the voice of the Lord one day telling him that the Father knew of his sufferings. This gave him the renewed courage to go on.

PRAYER

I praise you, Lord, for the deliverance that is in the name of Jesus. He has the keys of death and hell, and the power of his blood frees me from the evil one. He has rescued me from the kingdom of darkness and brought me into his marvellous light. Amen.

MEMORY VERSE

But on Mount Zion will be deliverance...

(Obadiah 17)

Jesus in Jonah

Jonah is mainly in narrative form as he runs away from God's call, gets swallowed by the great fish and ends up in Nineveh. He preaches about coming judgment and then is surprised when the people do repent and God has mercy. Jesus is seen in the book as:

- The mercy of God
- The one who was raised on the third day

The Mercy of God

Jonah was exasperated when God forgave the Assyrians. God taught him a lesson by causing a vine to grow to give him shade – then the vine withered. He will have mercy upon whom he will have mercy. Jesus is the mercy of God personified, the human face of God who stooped low to save us when we did not deserve it: 'But God demonstrates his own love for us in this: While we were still sinners, Christ died for us' (Romans 5:8).

My friend Kurt runs a ministry to the homeless in London, Besides a Sunday service, a ministry with drug addicts and the homeless in the week, he holds an open air service outside Westminster Cathedral in London, giving out drinks and sandwiches and then they pray. The regulars call this 'The Church without Walls'. He sees much mercy poured out on those who live broken lives, but one day, walking back from a time distributing food and clothes to the homeless, he passed a smartly dressed man standing by a bus stop. He felt the nudging of the Holy Spirit to stop and talk to him. Kurt hesitated as the man looked well off and all together. He did speak and the man was contemplating suicide. God, in his mercy, is no respecter of persons, but reaches out to those who are broken-hearted.

The One Who Was Raised on the Third Day

Jonah in the belly of the great fish for three days and nights is a type of Christ's resurrection. Jesus himself refers to Jonah in this way: 'For as Jonah was three days and three nights in the belly of a huge fish, so the Son of Man will be three days and three nights in the heart of the earth' (Matthew 12:40).

PRAYER
Father, I thank you for your undeserved mercy that was poured out on us through Jesus. When we were lost in sin, Christ died for us. He went through the darkness of death and on the third day he was raised up, taking us with him. Amen.

MEMORY VERSE

When God saw what they did and how they turned from their evil, he had compassion and did not bring upon them the destruction he had threatened.
(Jonah 3:10)

Jesus in Micah

Micah preached in the eighth century BC as a contemporary of Isaiah. He warned Judah to repent, as Assyria threatened to invade. His short book contains a vision of future peace on earth and an early form of messianic hope. Jesus is seen as:

- The peacemaker
- The ruler from Bethlehem

The Peacemaker

Micah's vision (Micah 4:1–5) of all nations coming to the mountain of the Lord and living in peace, beating swords into ploughshares, is a hope that has begun to be fulfilled in Jesus. He is the peacemaker between God and humanity: 'For he himself is our peace, who has made the two one and has destroyed the barrier, the dividing wall of hostility' (Ephesians 2:14); 'Therefore, since we have been justified through faith, we have peace with God through our Lord Jesus Christ' (Romans 5:1).

The Ruler from Bethlehem

But you, Bethlehem Ephrathah,
    though you are small among the clans of Judah,

> out of you will come for me
>> one who will be ruler over Israel,
> whose origins are from of old,
>> from ancient times. (Micah 5:2)

This amazing oracle pinpoints the small town of Bethlehem as a significant place in the history of salvation. It picks up on the oracle about a ruler coming from Judah in Genesis 49:10. This was fulfilled by the birth of Jesus, as his family returned to their hometown during a census. Matthew alludes to this oracle in the story of the magi (Matthew 2:3–8). Today Bethlehem is situated in the midst of the tensions in the Holy Land. The Church of the Nativity stands at the centre of Christian witness there with the traditional spot of the birth marked by a star on the ground. Pilgrims flock to this site and seek to kiss the ground out of reverence. If this is truly the spot, then you can understand such respect being paid. It is akin to flowers and messages left beside hedges or roads where someone died in a car accident. Some places just contain precious memories. I remember once seeing a sketch made by a soldier during World War II. Several of his colleagues were kneeling, kissing the ground or just looking. What thoughts must have passed through their minds as they contemplated the birth of the Prince of Peace amidst the war.

The statement about his origin being from ancient times (literally 'from days of eternity') could mean that he was prophesied about many centuries ago (hence Jacob's words in Genesis) or that he was in existence in the beginning as the pre-existent Christ. An intriguing and enigmatic verse.

PRAYER

Thank you, Lord, that Jesus is our peace and that he has removed the dividing wall between us. Thank you that his birth was prophesied many centuries ago, and that you honoured the clans of Judah. Thank you that we can trust your word. Amen.

MEMORY VERSE

They will beat their swords into ploughshares and their spears into pruning hooks. Nation will not take up sword against nation, nor will they train for war any more.   (Micah 4:3)

Jesus in Nahum

Nahum prophesied that Nineveh of the Assyrians would fall, as it did in 612 BC. Jesus is seen in this short book as:

* The avenger of the people

The Avenger of the People

The Lord is a jealous and avenging God;...
    the Lord takes vengeance on his foes
    and maintains his wrath against his enemies.

(Nahum 1:2)

God is merciful but just, and sins will be punished if not forgiven and injustice will be overthrown. Jesus showed incredible mercy but could be firm and fierce at times. In the story of his early preaching in the synagogues of Capernaum, he shuts up an evil spirit and speaks to it curtly and sternly (see Mark 1:21–28). I was studying this passage with our Men's Group when some of them, relatively unchurched, expressed surprise at Jesus' sternness. They are a motley crew, a pleasant bunch of blokes, the typical 'Grumpy Old Men' who revel in nostalgia and have a moan about many things in today's society. I had to explain that Jesus was acting sharply, nipping trouble in the bud. He also overturned the money-changers' tables in the Temple in disgust. Jesus was not just gentle, meek and mild. He could be tough and feisty. Jesus is also the coming judge when the earth will shake and the stars will fall. Read through Revelation 19:1–21 to get a poetic glimpse of this coming sifting and shaking: '...He treads the winepress of the fury of the wrath of God Almighty. On his robe and on his thigh he has this name written: KING OF KINGS AND LORD OF LORDS' (Revelation 19:15–16).

'Vengeance is mine,' says the Lord... we are to forgive and hand over our hurts and injustices to the Father. He will be the righter of wrongs. I heard a Jew describing a scene he had witnessed; a grandfather holding his grandson in Auschwitz just before they were shot; vengeance and righteousness belongs to the Lord. These things have to be paid back.

PRAYER
Father, I bow before you, remembering that you are our judge and avenger. You will bring justice on earth and heal the hurts of your people. Thank you that the coming judge still bears the scars of the nails and the wound in his side. You are a God who loves us and we can find shelter under your wings. Amen.

MEMORY VERSE

The Lord is a jealous and an avenging God.
(Nahum 1:2)

Jesus in Habakkuk

Habakkuk was a contemporary of Jeremiah who also prophesied the fall of Jerusalem. Jesus is seen as:

- God my saviour
- The one who goes on high

God my Saviour

yet I will rejoice in the Lord,
  I will be joyful in God my Saviour.   (Habakkuk 3:18)

Despite all the calamities that are to come upon Judah and Jerusalem, Habakkuk ends on an upbeat note. God is saviour and will not finally abandon his people. Jesus means 'God is Saviour' and he brings the saving power of God to earth in his person.

Habakkuk also has a theophany, an appearance of God in glory and majesty:

… His glory covered the heavens
  and his praise filled the earth.
His splendour was like the sunrise;
  rays flashed from his hand,
  where his power was hidden. (Habakkuk 3:3–4)

This is the Jesus of the transfiguration or of the opening chapter of Revelation. Each experience of awe at the beauty of life is a hint of that transcendent glory. I remember watching the blossoms on an apple tree for minutes when a boy, transfixed by their colour and beauty. I had a strong sense of life flowing through the tree, the blossom and myself. It was a tiny, brief mystical experience. Such moments that take the breath away open our spirits and minds up to the Glory.

The One Who Goes on High

The Sovereign Lord is my strength;
> he makes my feet like the feet of a deer,
> he enables me to go on the heights.   (Habakkuk 3:19)

The prophet was strengthened by the Lord and lifted out of potential gloom. He felt that this strength could lead him to the heights, like a deer skipping and climbing a mountain. This is a Near Eastern image of skill and strength. Apart from the grace of God at work, we see a hint of Jesus here, for he was the one who ascended on high: 'Since, then, you have been raised with Christ, set your hearts on things above, where Christ is seated at the right hand of God' (Colossians 3:1). At the end of this section in Habakkuk, God is hailed by the title 'Saviour'.

PRAYER

Father, I praise you that you are my saviour and that you come in power to my aid. Thank you for your strength and grace, that I have ascended on high in Christ and am seated in heavenly places with him. Amen.

MEMORY VERSE

Yet I will rejoice in the Lord, I will be joyful in God my Saviour. (Habakkuk 3:18)

Jesus in Zephaniah

Zephaniah prophesied in the seventh century, in the reign of King Josiah. Jesus is seen as:

• The Lord is mighty to save

The Lord is Mighty to Save

The Lord your God is with you,
 he is mighty to save.
He will take great delight in you,
 he will quiet you with his love,
 he will rejoice over you with singing.

(Zephaniah 3:17)

A beautiful passage that reveals the heart of God, and this is fulfilled in Jesus as saviour and Lord. As 'Immanuel', 'God with us', the rejoicing, saving love engulfs us in his presence. It is so easy to be hung up on being unworthy and thinking of God as distant. There is so much in the New Testament about God's rejoicing over us when we come to him. By the Holy Spirit, we can cry out, '*Abba*, Father' after all (see Romans 8:15)! The experience of praising him in tongues – languages unlearned – is a rising up of love and rejoicing, sometimes in heavenly song. The preacher Mahesh Chavdah describes this gift as the bridal language of the kingdom. It is the language of intimacy. The experience of communal singing in tongues is holy ground. You are singing with the angels, tasting the worship of heaven. Yet, without this gift, we can still know that he rejoices over us through the Holy Spirit. It moves me greatly when I sense a desire to sing in tongues over someone who comes to me for prayer. The Spirit rejoices over them.

PRAYER

Thank you, Lord, that you rejoice over me with singing, that you surround me with your love and that I can call you my Father. Amen.

MEMORY VERSE

The Lord your God is with you,
    he is mighty to save. (Zephaniah 3:17)

Jesus in Haggai

Haggai returned to Jerusalem after the fall of Babylon and prophesied there about the coming king and the rebuilding of the Temple. Jesus is seen as:

- The restorer
- The new temple
- The signet ring

The Restorer

God stirs up certain people, Zerubbabel and Joshua the high priest, to restore the house of the Lord. Then their fortunes will be reversed and blessings will be restored. 'From this day on I will bless you' (Haggai 2:19). In the new covenant we have every spiritual blessing. 'Praise be to the God and Father of our Lord Jesus Christ, who has blessed us in the heavenly realms with every spiritual blessing in Christ' (Ephesians 1:3).

The New Temple

The Lord promises that the glory of the new temple will be greater than that of the former: ' "... I will fill this house with glory," says the Lord... "And in this place I will grant peace" ' (Haggai 2:7, 9). Jesus is the real fulfilment of this as the new Temple, filled with all the fullness of God. This is the reason for his magnetism, his attraction. This was once compared to the attraction a large community bonfire has to people of all social types and ages. They gather and start to draw closer to the warmth and the light.

The Signet Ring

The Lord tells Zerubbabel, '... I will make you like my signet ring, for I have chosen you...' (Haggai 2:23). This is a choice of a new king, an anointed one. It is part of the messianic cycle, for each king is a messiah. Jesus is the chosen one, the anointed one par excellence. Any believer who feels a call and a blessing upon their lives knows this sense of special honour but there is often grit, determination and struggle involved. There is always some level of cost involved and some will not make the course. The Pentecostal healer Kathryn Kulman used to claim that many men had been called to her calling but had refused the cost until she accepted. Or, again, when I read of the determination and the struggles of Rory and Wendy Alec to found GOD TV in the UK and then to broadcast around the globe, I was moved by their faith and perseverance.

PRAYER
I praise you, Lord, that you desire to give us every spiritual blessing in Jesus – that this is our right and inheritance. Thank you that we are filled with your glory in his presence and that we are anointed with his Spirit. Amen.

MEMORY VERSE

I will make you like my signet ring, for I have chosen you.
(Haggai 2:23)

Jesus in Zechariah

Zechariah was a contemporary of Haggai, a returning exile. He used exotic imagery and some of the same apocalyptic style that is found in Daniel. Jesus is seen as:

- The Branch
- The fountain
- The wounded shepherd

The Branch

Joshua the high priest is given a Messianic title, 'the Branch': 'Here is the man whose name is the Branch, and he will branch out from his place and build the temple of the Lord' (Zechariah 6:12). This led to speculations that there would be two messiahs, a priestly one and a royal one. Jesus combined both roles as we see in Hebrews as the Messiah and the high priest. Joshua and any other man of God up to the coming of Jesus had a share in the messianic anointing and could have titles applied to him, such as 'the Branch'. Jesus is the real Branch, though, the true fulfilment.

The Fountain

'On that day a fountain will be opened to the house of David and the inhabitants of Jerusalem, to cleanse them from sin and impurity' (Zechariah 13:1). The cleansing fountain is seen flowing from the side of Jesus on the cross as blood and water flowed from his wound. The Catholic devotion of the Divine Mercy, begun by a Polish nun, St Faustina, which I have mentioned before, picks up on this as the risen Lord is pictured with a flash of red and white light striking us from his side. In this fountain we are cleansed, forgiven and loved. Such imagery is found in Protestant hymnology, too:

> There is a fountain filled with blood
> drawn from Emmanuel's veins;
> and sinners, plunged beneath that flood,
> lose all their guilty stains.   (William Cowper, 1731–1800)

The Wounded Shepherd

... Strike the shepherd and the sheep will be scattered,
and I will turn my hand against the little ones.

(Zechariah 13:7)

This enigmatic verse echoes that of the suffering servant in Isaiah 53. God's man is struck down and the people flee. This is another hint of a suffering Messiah that was fulfilled in the Passion of Christ.

PRAYER

Thank you, Father, that Jesus is our high priest and our King, that we can be cleansed under the fountain of his blood, that he was wounded for us. Amen.

MEMORY VERSE

On that day a fountain will be opened to the house of David and the inhabitants of Jerusalem, to cleanse them from sin and impurity.   (Zechariah 13:1)

Jesus in Malachi

Malachi was probably a contemporary of Ezra and Nehemiah and prophesied to the returning exiles. Jesus is seen in:

- The refiner
- The sun of righteousness
- The pure offering

The Refiner

'... Then suddenly the Lord you are seeking will come to his temple; the messenger of the covenant, whom you desire, will come' (Malachi 3:1). When the Lord comes, he will come as a refiner: '... Who can stand when he appears? For he will be like a refiner's fire...' (Malachi 3:2). This is the one whom John the Baptist said would baptize with the Holy Spirit and with fire. This is the sender of the Holy Spirit who sanctifies his people (see John 14:15–17). It is said that a refiner of precious metal will sit and watch the melted metal until he can see his face in it clearly. If the heat is turned on any longer it will spoil. That is purity, to see the refiner's face in the silver. The Holy Spirit is pledged to refine us until the face of Christ is seen through ours.

We can all know moments of the refiner's touch, but

the most holy encounter I have ever had with the Lord was on a retreat in Ars in France recently. One morning, during worship, I was on my knees when I felt wave after wave of intense holiness sweeping over me. I laughed, cried, shook, and stayed firmly on my knees. The divine surgeon was at work then and there and I am still unpacking what was happening. I got up at the end and could hardly walk, feeling like an astronaut walking on the moon. My legs were like jelly!

Going back to the Bible, we can see a level of fulfilment of the text of Malachi in the story of the presentation in the Temple recorded in Luke 2:21–40) The elderly Simeon and the prophetess Anna recognized the Lord in their midst; he had suddenly come into his Temple.

The Sun of Righteousness

'But for you who revere my name, the sun of righteousness will rise with healing in its wings' (Malachi 4:2). This image is suggestive of the resurrection, of the risen, victorious Christ. His atoning death has brought healing power to his church:

> But he was pierced for our transgressions,
>   he was crushed for our iniquities;
> the punishment that brought us peace was upon him,
>   and by his wounds we are healed.   (Isaiah 53:5)

The Pure Offering

My name will be great among the nations, from the rising to the setting of the sun. In every place incense and pure offerings will be brought to my name, because my name will be great among the nations...   (Malachi 1:11)

This pure offering can be seen as the spiritual sacrifice of praise upon the lips of the redeemed, whatever the nationality, for '... with your blood you purchased men for God from every tribe and language and people and nation' (Revelation 5:9).

The early church also saw this as a prophecy about the offering of the eucharist each week. This is a sacrifice of praise and a memorial of Christ's pure offering. As early as the *Didache*, a list of teachings and liturgy from the first century AD, this link was being made. It is possible that some of the apostles were still alive when this was written.

PRAYER

Father, I thank you for your refining fire. Purify my heart. May Jesus rise as the sun of righteousness over me with healing in his wings, for by his wounds am I healed. Thank you that we can offer you worthy praise with our lips and join together in the memorial of Jesus' pure offering as we share bread and wine. Amen.

MEMORY VERSE

But for you who revere my name, the sun of righteousness will rise with healing in its wings.

(Malachi 4:2)

The Hope of Israel

Ancient Prejudice

I once took a school party of fourteen-year-olds to the Anne Frank House in Amsterdam. It was a moving experience as we made our way around this typical, bourgeois Dutch house. The part that struck the young people the most was the room that Anne had slept in. On the wall there are still the pictures she had pinned to the wall, many taken out of magazines. They were stars and pinups of her day. A sheet of plexiglas covers these to preserve them. Just before you leave, visitors go through a final room where there are displays, interactive consoles and visitors' books. I had never seen the young people so cowed, quiet and thoughtful as they signed a few comments, took a last look at this and that and then began to file out.

Anne Frank's story is tragic, part of a horrible tapestry of anti-Semitism through the ages. Sadly, the medieval church fuelled the prejudice by calling all Jews 'Christ killers' and accusing them of deicide. This might have been corrected and renounced, but until relatively recently such folk beliefs were still in circulation. Helen Shapiro, the singer, is now a Messianic Jew. She has told how as a girl aged six others would scold her in the playground for killing Jesus. She hadn't even heard of Jesus, let alone done anything to hurt him! This was brought home to me as an Anglican seminarian when I was walking through the backstreets of Manchester during a bus strike. I had a long black coat on as it was December, and a black hat. In those days I also sported a beard. Suddenly, a group of children who were playing in the street started shouting at me.

'Yid lid! Yid lid! You crucified the Lord Jesus, you did!'

They had mistaken me for an orthodox Jew, despite the red shoes I was also sporting! Shocking, and this was in 1986!

Prejudice can linger on. I glimpsed this recently in the movie *The Passion of the Christ*. This was a powerful movie that communicated aspects of the gospel to many people, but one detail was disturbing (sorry, Mel!), and a detail that I have not seen anyone else mention. The portrayal of Barabbas was flawed, in my view. He appeared as a gibbering, almost mad, murderer, 'the mad axe-man' of his day. This follows a tradition that goes back through to medieval mystery plays where to show him as a mad killer threw more blame on the Jews. How could they have chosen this man rather than their Messiah? It is more likely that Barabbas was a terrorist, a freedom-fighter. Jesus seemed to have failed in the eyes of many of the people. He had not resisted arrest. At least Barabbas had taken up arms and tried to do something! This is uncertain, but likely (see Mark 15:7 where Barabbas is not a murderer, but one of a group of insurrectionists who had resisted the Romans).

Fulfilment or Replacement?

All of this writing about the Old Testament Scriptures and how Jesus fulfilled them or was predicted in them might lead to a Jewish theological cul-de-sac. If it has all been fulfilled and Messiah has come, then has it been set aside and replaced by something else (Christianity or the church)? Some do teach this, and speak of 'replacement theology' where the church has replaced Israel in all the promises in the Old Testament and all the blessings and desires of God's heart. Speaking as an Anglican, this is quite common in my own Church, though there are various perspectives on Israel. Whilst many might be pro-Jewish, they baulk at any ongoing significance of the land. Prophecies about this (all Old Testament) are seen as symbols of spiritual blessing in the Church today. I used to think this but now I am not so sure. There have been far more extreme attempts to jettison the Old Testament in Christian history, such as the views of Marcion in the second century AD. He argued that a different God was behind the Old Testament, and Jesus had revealed a Higher God. His views were influenced by aspects of the Greek philosophy of his day and esoteric movements. Quite rightly, his views were denounced by the church as heretical. But replacement theology? What is needed is a fulfilment theology that does not jettison Israel.

Reading the New Testament shows us that Israel still has a place in God's heart, alongside the existence of the church. A key passage is Romans 11. Let us have a look at this carefully.

'Did God reject his people? By no means!' states Paul (verse 1). They still have a place in his heart and they are not condemned because Jesus was crucified in ignorance (and it was ignorance – check out 1 Corinthians 2:8). He develops the argument in verse 11: 'Again I ask: Did they stumble so as to fall beyond recovery? Not at all! Rather, because of their transgression, salvation has come to the Gentiles to make Israel envious.'

As they turned from the gospel as a whole, then the door was opened for the Gentiles to enter. Of course, the first Christians were Jews. Jesus was a Jew. The first pope (i.e. St Peter) was a Jew. But the Jews as a whole turned away. Jesus was seen as a failed Messiah for a crucified saviour was folly (see 1 Corinthians 1:21–23). It is almost as though Paul argues that they had to turn away, to reject, so that others might believe. I have heard this put, movingly, that it is like having to accept the rejection of your own children to see salvation come to other families down the street. You rejoice that the others are saved but you still love, pray for and yearn for your own. Paul adds: 'But if their transgression means riches for the world, and their loss means riches for the Gentiles, how much greater riches will their fulness bring!' (Romans 11:12).

Again, he adds: 'For if their rejection is the reconciliation of the world, what will their acceptance be but life from the dead?' (Romans 11:15).

These are intriguing, eschatological ideas. The end times will mean a turning to the gospel for the Jews and great blessing will come upon them. Paul goes on: '... Israel has experienced a hardening in part until the full number of the Gentiles has come in. And so all Israel shall be saved...' (Romans 11:25–26) – he also reminds us that the Gentiles are grafted into the olive tree of ancient Israel. We are not the root but branches: '... You do not support the root, but the root supports you' (Romans 11:18).

Another analogy is the Old Testament offering of the firstfruits. The part of the dough that was offered was considered holy – i.e. Israel – then the whole batch is set apart as holy food, to be consumed by the priests in the Temple. It could not be common food again (see Leviticus 6:14–18). Thus, if Israel is holy, then so are Gentile believers in the Messiah: '... if the root is holy, so are the branches' (Romans 11:16).

Finally, Paul declares that the gifts of God are without repentance: 'for God's gifts and his call are irrevocable' (Romans 11:29). He adds: '... they are loved on account of the patriarchs' (Romans 11:28).

We are grateful to Israel for the covenant, for the patriarchs and for the Messiah. We owe them much, and God has not finished with the people of Israel yet. They have a role and a part in his plan of salvation for the future, not just the past.

The Land and Jerusalem?

The people are one thing, but the land and the city of Jerusalem are another concern. What are we to make of all the promises about the land? This is a highly charged political question because of Palestinian concerns. Replacement theology wants to change all promises about the land or Jerusalem to the church in general. It must be said, though, that no one denies the Jews the right to a homeland of some kind after all they have gone through in the past. It is a question of rights and boundaries.

This is a complicated, historical problem and no amount of study seems to lighten this matter or unravel the tricky knots of claims and counterclaims. The history of this part of the Middle East is not easy to grasp in a hurry. What I can say, with all confidence, is that if the people of God still have a call upon them and a place in God's heart, then so does the land of his choice and blessing. It is hard to dismiss this when reading the Old Testament. It is true that some aspects of prophecies about the land can be applied to the church as a blessing upon all God's people, and some oracles about a new Exodus and a restoration after the exile in Babylon can only be seen as fulfilled in Jesus. Through him there is a great ingathering across the whole world (e.g. Haggai 2:7–9 and the final chapters of Isaiah). But the actual land is still there. It is a physical reality and the gifts and call of God are irrevocable. We are encouraged, commanded, to pray for the peace of Jerusalem:

> Pray for the peace of Jerusalem:
>> 'May those who love you be secure.
> May there be peace within your walls
>> and security within your citadels.'
> For the sake of my brothers and friends,
>> I will say, 'Peace be within you.'   (Psalm 122:6–8)

> If I forget you, O Jerusalem,
>> may my right hand forget its skill.
> May my tongue cling to the roof of my mouth,
>> if I do not remember you,
> if I do not consider Jerusalem my highest joy.
>>>>   (Psalm 137:5–6)

Jerusalem, the city that stands on Mount Zion, holy and sanctified by the presence of the Temple, has a role in the end times, too:

In the last days
the mountain of the Lord's temple will be established
    as chief among the mountains;
it will be raised above the hills,
    and all nations will stream to it.
Many peoples will come and say,
    'Come, let us go up to the mountain of the Lord,
    to the house of the God of Jacob.
    He will teach us his ways,
    so that we may walk in his paths.'
    The law will go out from Zion,
    The word of the Lord from Jerusalem. (Isaiah 2:2–3)

There is a huge debate about the rebuilding of the Temple. Some predict this and pray for it within the church as a fulfilment of various Old Testament prophecies such as Ezekiel 47. However, if Jesus is the new Temple, and we are all living stones within this Temple (see 1 Peter 2:5), then will a new, physical one be rebuilt? Would it have any significance? Is this not a red herring? I have no answers to this. I merely throw out the question.

But Jerusalem has a destiny, and that is clear from the Scriptures. There is much I do not claim to know, or have the answers to. I have the great pleasure of a new friendship with a hilarious, big-hearted Messianic Jew and I am prepared to learn much more at his feet.

What about Palestine?

When we enter the realm of rights for the Palestinians things get complicated and we see the claims and counterclaims. There is a place for the land under Israel with Jerusalem as the capital. There are also human beings who live there who are not Israel, and some of them have lived there for generations. It is true that there was no Palestinian nation in the past. It is a modern creation. There were people, though. Some have only lived there for a short time, for a generation or two. Some have lived there for generations, dating back to the Roman times. For many centuries, people travelled across this land as nomadic tribes, but there were settled communities. And some of these people were forcibly removed when Israel was established as a nation. There *were* refugees from fighting that broke out because the Arab nations attacked and tried to wipe out Israel. There were also villages that were evicted or even massacred. Maybe this was by break-away, terrorist Jewish groups rather than people under official army command. But it happened. The Palestinians have been placed in camps or in restricted regions, frustrated and with few rights. Yes, we have seen terrorism and uprisings, the horror of suicide bombings and Muslim extremism stirring up hatred. There will always be, and there have always been, those who will refuse to recognize Israel. This is a spiritual matter for the enemy will rise up against the righteous seed. However, Israel does not have completely clean hands. To support Israel and its right to exist does not mean that everything they do is right. There is extremism on their side, and gross secularism, too. Women serving in the army, for example, are allowed two free abortions as promiscuity is so rife. There is arrogance and some of the political problems have been inflamed by their attitudes.

There can be awkward characteristics. A friend of mine works with a charity that collects clothes for Jews who are recent immigrants. Some of these people come from poor backgrounds – Russian Jews leaving a deprived, post-communist lifestyle behind or Ethiopian Jews who do not have the capital or skills to make it on their own. Their plight is not always admitted by Israel's media or foreign relations team. It is a small country without the infrastructure or sound economy to support all the poorer people coming to settle. They have a right to settle, to make *aliya* as they are Jews. True, but there are problems.

She told me about her culture shock when first going to Israel. She got on a bus with a girlfriend. Her friend sat down and then there was only one seat free next to an Orthodox Jewish man. He deliberately placed his grocery bags on the seat. After a while, the seat opposite became free. She sat down and the man took out a fountain pen from his top pocket and carefully placed it by her seat, in between them. As the bus pulled away, the pen rolled down the aisle. She bent down and offered it to him. He froze, awkwardly, and so she simply placed it on the groceries. Afterwards this was explained to her. As an Orthodox Jew he had to sit separately from a woman, particularly a Gentile woman. The fountain pen was a symbolic screen. She felt anger and revulsion, even if she did not want to.

I heard a speaker at a conference describing his visit to Israel and seeing Jewish residents callously throwing their dirty water out over a balcony on a road where many Palestinians lived, as people walked by. He said, 'I want to support Israel. I am an evangelical Christian, but how can I support that kind of behaviour?'

Another friend of mine had been working in the Anglican cathedral in Cairo. He was flying to the UK when the plane had to land in Israel because of some trouble. He and others who had an Egyptian visa in their passports were separated, made to wait, treated with contempt, and one woman was made to open her case. The soldiers mocked and insulted her and my friend, a priest, stood up for her. They seized his case and told him that he would never see it again. He didn't.

These attitudes are plain wrong and are inexcusable. But they are God's people. His gifts and call are irrevocable. We don't have to like everyone in that gifting and calling, but we have to honour and support them. We can also criticize, though, and not whitewash.

Perhaps prayer for Israel should include a call to repentance and spiritual renewal for the Jews. They need to wash their hands. Remember that God spared Jerusalem from the threat of the Assyrians when King Hezekiah humbled himself and led the people in repentance (2 Kings 18–19).

I have read three books recently that have crystallized the issues for me. The first was *Light Force*[1] by Brother Andrew. This was the man who once smuggled Bibles into Russia. His latest book chronicles his adventures in Lebanon and Israel. He is pro-Israel without a doubt, but his time spent helping Lebanese Christians' and Palestinian Christians opened his eyes to the plight of the Arabs. He gained the confidence of many Muslims, too, and treated them with the utmost respect and courtesy whilst not compromising his own faith. He grew to love them as 'Godfearers', a term used in New Testament times for searching Gentiles, seeking the one, true, living God. He has been instrumental in setting up meetings between Palestinian Christians and Messianic Jews.

---

1 Brother Andrew with Al Janssen, *Light Force*, Grand Rapids, MI: Chosen Books, 2004.

The second book is *Blood Brothers*[2] by Father Elias Chacour. Father Elias is a Melkite Catholic priest and a Palestinian. He is held in high regard by his own people, including the Muslims. He tells a moving story of his childhood when his village was evacuated by Israeli forces (it is often asserted that these would have been renegade, bandit groups by modern Israelis) and a neighbouring one was massacred. His family never returned to their house. He lived with Jews and Muslims peacefully in his youth, and is not against Israel. He does question extreme and triumphant forms of Zionism, though, and issues a challenge to Christians to examine the biblical prophecies about the return of Israel. This will be eschatological and a great blessing for all. For example, a restored Israel will be a 'banner for the nations' (Isaiah 11:12), and the Lord will show that he is holy through Israel (Ezekiel 36:23) – it is for the sake of the Lord's name that he will gather Israel again, for a witness to the world (Ezekiel 36:22–23). Father Elias asks if that return has really happened. Perhaps it has just started, but many aspects of prophecy have yet to be fulfilled and we need to see the holiness and righteousness of God sweeping through the nation. He has a point there. But Israel has a right to be and must be prayed for, let us not forget. Our prayers are that the refiner's fire will be at work, that the name will be honoured, and Israel's behaviour will be a banner for the nations.

The third book is by a secular Jew, *The Other Side of Israel*[3] by Susan Nathan. She chose to live in an all Arab

---

2 Father Elias Chacour, *Blood Brothers*, Grand Rapids, MI: Chosen Books, 1984.

3 Susan Nathan, *The Other Side of Israel*, London: Harper Collins Publishers Ltd., 2005.

town within the borders of Israel. She went through the upheaval of moving from Tel Aviv with all its facilities to Tamra in the Galilee region. She rejects the prejudice of some of her own people and finds the Arab Israelis down to earth, honest and possessed of a great family, communal life. She has been semi-adopted by the family she rents rooms from and is under the protection of their tribe. She can take forever walking down the street to shop as so many stop and talk, inviting her for coffee. It is an eye-opener and a reminder of the blind spots and faults to be found on both sides. She points out that Israel is operating a form of apartheid. Things are now so tense and defensive that it is hard to see how this can unravel.

Despite all the problems and shortfalls, the Jews are still God's people. They are not always right, sometimes completely wrong, but they are his people.

Messianic Judaism or the Church?

Another debate that rages today is about Messianic Judaism. Converted Jews wish to remain Jews and worship in a Jewish way. So they form separate congregations, Messianic synagogues with rabbis and not priests or ministers. They use Hebrew chant and liturgy, keep the Jewish festivals, meet on the Sabbath (Saturday), follow the Torah food laws, but they believe in Jesus. I have seen some examples of Messianic worship and I am impressed. It has influenced my approach to worship – a mixture of informality, modern praise and set liturgy. Their styles will vary from congregation to congregation. Some can be stand-offish, isolated from the church. Some see themselves as somewhat superior, the 'real thing', as they are still immersed in their Jewish roots. Some Christian groups are arguing that we should become more Jewish, we should keep festivals like Tabernacles or Yom Kippur, or even switch holy days to Saturday. Others want them to stop doing their own thing and join established churches.

Surely it is all a matter of balance. It is wise and understandable that converted Jews want to retain their cultural identity as far as possible. They can also be a living witness to other Jews for whom the established churches are a bridge too far. They can keep the ritual laws if they wish, so long as this is voluntary as Paul did (see Acts 21:26). We can keep any of the festivals if we so desire. We have that right and that is our inheritance. However, we are Gentile believers and grafted onto the tree. The same ritual obligations are not placed upon us (hence many passages in Paul; see also Acts 15:19–21). Furthermore, the Lord's Day (i.e. Sunday as the first day of the week and the day of the resurrection) is biblical and a venerable, ancient tradition (see Revelation 1:10). Honouring the Jews and Israel does not mean trying to cease to be Gentile believers.

In conclusion…

I haven't got any slick answers to offer for the Palestinian problem. They are human beings made in the image of God. But Israel has a right to security and self-defence as well as needing to love the stranger in the gate. It's a mess, all tangled up in violence and fear. Maybe there will be no answers, or no complete answers, until the Lord returns. A spiritual problem exists besides a political one and that needs a spiritual answer. What can be done to defuse things in the meantime must be done. But the Jews are the Lord's people, and his gifts and callings are without repentance.

God told Abraham:

I will bless those who bless you,
    and whoever curses you I will curse... (Genesis 12:3)

So we bless his people, and yet we are also children of Abraham spiritually, by adoption through Christ: 'He redeemed us in order that the blessing given to Abraham might come to the Gentiles through Christ Jesus, so that by faith we might receive the promise of the Spirit' (Galatians 3:14).

We belong to each other. We have been grafted onto the olive tree.

APPENDIX 2:
Oracles about Jesus

Many types and images that are suggestive of Jesus have been traced and studied in this book. They are interesting and edifying, but it might be useful to isolate, clearly, precise oracles. There are prophecies about the coming of Jesus that are meant to be so, that are looking into the future, rather than revealing symbols or revelations of the nature of God which we see so clearly in the face of Jesus.

- Genesis 3:15 – the woman's offspring will defeat the serpent
- Genesis 49:10 – a ruler will come from Judah
- Numbers 24:17 – promise of a ruler and a star shall rise
- 2 Samuel 7:13–14 – a promised son who will reign for ever
- Psalm 22:14–18 – prediction of the Passion
- Isaiah 7:14 – the virgin birth
- Isaiah 9:2–7 – the promised child who is Prince of Peace and Mighty God
- Isaiah 11:1–9 – the child will bring in the kingdom of God
- Isaiah 53 – The suffering servant
- Jeremiah 23:5 – prophecy of the Branch
- Daniel 7:13 – the coming of the Son of man

- Micah 5:2 – a ruler from Bethlehem
- Zechariah 13 – a fountain shall rise in Israel
- Zechariah 13:7 – the wounded shepherd